At the Chalkface

Great Moments in Education

At the Chalkface

Great Moments in Education

by
Ian Whitwham

TEACH
BOOKS

Published by Hopscotch
Teach Books Division, MA Education Ltd, St Jude's Church, Dulwich Road, London
SE24 0PB

British Library Cataloguing-in-Publication Data
A catalogue record is available for this book

ISBN-13: 978 1 90539 099 1

Printed by CLE, St Ives, Huntingdon, Cambridgeshire

Contents

Acknowledgements

Many thanks to Mark Allen for thinking that these columns would be a good idea and to perfect editors Pete Henshaw and Rebecca Linssen. Thanks also to all those pupils who have endured my lessons over the years, to all those Crumlins presently toiling in our classrooms. And, especially, to the darling girls Jill, Anna and Alice.

Dedicated to Nigel Molesworth who stil kno

Introduction

You've just done a six-lesson day. You've also phoned Ronald Crumlin's mum, met Sidney Lunk's social worker and checked Cordelia Swansong's Oxbridge statement. You've lined up the antic 7th year for lunch, explored the Metaphysicals with the whizzo 13th year, trawled through conditionals with the bonkers 8th year and quelled a minor riot in the playground. You've had consultants in your classrooms with clipboards with enough criteria to sink Socrates himself. You've failed some foggy targets and suffered ultimatums in grim dawn briefings.

And that's not all.

Tabloid hacks and broadsheet scribes attack you and your pupils and all that state schools stand for. The 'broken society', grocers' plurals, chlamydia, happy slapping and original sin are probably your fault. They are joined by gesture politicians and assorted pundits, who have rarely been in a state school classroom and pay thousand of pounds a year for their children to avoid the kind pupils you teach. Who is it this week? Big Ed Balls or Screaming Lord Woodentop or The Boy Gove or the Dread Melanie Phillips? Or is it a Respect Czar? A Fat Czar? A Drug Czar? A Foreplay Czar? A Condom Czar.

What a confederacy of dunces!

If you didn't laugh you'd weep.

You ponder bunking off another twilight workshop with another PowerPoint clot talking about another set of targets. You slump into the staffroom and pick up *SecEd*. 'At the Chalkface'. What's this? Not another droning bore telling you how to do it! Not another guru with a humour bypass droning on!

Well, I hope not. These pieces are meant to cheer you up. To celebrate teachers and pupils most of whom seem to me honourable, decent, talented, industrious and richly witty.

I've taught for over 30 years in inner city comprehensives. Mostly in the 'Eton of comprehensives' – as it is still quaintly labelled. We went, like many schools, from a thrilling, creative haven to a modish, strict exam regime. Dithering old liberals *vs* strict modern managers. We got stuffed. These pieces reflect those culture wars. The section divisions are, inevitably, a little arbitrary. The experience of the classroom blurs such clumsy distinctions.

All these pieces have been published in *SecEd* since its launch in 2003. It has always let me be as silly or serious as I wished. It has always given teachers a real voice and I thank it for never stifling mine.

Ian Whitwham
London

Foreword

The best education columnist in the UK writes not for a blousy broadsheet. Nor does he write for a venture-capitalist owned trade journal. No. The most astute, most readable and consistently entertaining education columnist in the country writes for the weekly free-sheet that sits, sometimes still wrapped in its cellophane cover, on a table in the (soon to be disappeared) staffroom. His name is Ian Whitwham and he writes every week for a newspaper called *SecEd*: a newspaper that, as soon as it appears, I grab, rip the cellophane and greedily devour his latest postcard from where it counts.

Ian Whitwham has been for many, many years a hopelessly idealistic English teacher at a comp in inner city London. He is of a generation who saw teaching as a subversive political activity, who wanted to change the world; and there will be many cretinous functionaries in the upper echelons of the education management racket (none of whom will read this book) who would regard his burning love for his subject and generous, grand and glorious passion for the life chances of his pupils, as being the mutterings of an anachronism. Careerist fools all. Teaching is the only profession in which the laws of physics are suspended: the cream stays at the bottom. And Ian is, to use one of their favourite pieces of facile jargon, a perfect 'exemplar' of this law. He has (and is) a pulsating soul. A little tired, perhaps. But worth all the more for that fact.

This anthology is quite easily the best teaching memoir ever published. It will make you laugh out loud seven times within the space of first chapter, and if you are able to read Ian's lament for the freedom of sixth formers to be 'bohemian' without weeping salt tears for the wilfully brainless and systemic destruction of everything that was ever precious, then you are currently, probably spending too much of your working life processing data, pretending that this is teaching. It isn't. Teaching is a lifelong passion. Ian Whitwham has it.

Phil Beadle
Another schoolteacher

Chapter 1

In the classroom

'Is this a lesson, sir?'

All God's children are out there. Coming at you all the time. Thirty of them still in small Victorian classrooms. They bounce through the curriculum like balls in a pinball machine. From soil erosion to the Ten Commandments to photosynthesis to condoms to resistant materials to sponge cakes to great lakes and now to conditionals with me. No wonder they're dazed and confused.

"This is driving me bleedin' mental, sir!"

"Who he?"

Indeed. Who am I up there before them? Taking registers, having aims and intentions and detentions and plenaries, swooning about similes or barking at Shaka to get his dreadlocks out of the fan?

"Chill your beans, sir!"

Why do I keep yelling "right" at them and then glaring and then doing nothing? Sometimes I seem to be having soliloquies in a parallel universe. Or to have become invisible. Should I inscribe an arrow on the board pointing to me – "Your Teacher –Wigwam!" You must be all things to all pupils. Boss, shrink, stand up, cop, priest and scholar. Bore them and you're toast.

When it's good it's the best job on earth.

It's good with the tinies and the upper school. Most of the time.

When it's bad it's the worst.

I still can't do low-stream 8th years. I do all the proper stuff. Distance, boundaries, gravitas. I'm firm but fair. I don't smile 'til Christmas. To little avail. At best we settle for a low learning. At worst I have the Eno's effect. I prompt fizzing energies. The class resembles a car boot sale. Then I lose my temper and look like a boiled owl and then they laugh and smell blood. We settle for a truce. I try to get them with ruthless empathy, tough love and Beano humour.

It can drive you mental!

The Dread turns Macbeth to mayhem

Published 3 April 2003

A rare hush of intellectual curiosity – it might be dull torpor – hangs over the ninth year. We are knee deep in Macbeth.

A hacksaw voice rends the air.

"Sir! Sir! Look! Look! It's coming our way!"

Sabrina is at volume 11.

I keep calm.

"It is though, sir! It's getting lower!"

She'll do anything to avoid work. She gazes out of the window. I stay calm. We must get back to SATs. It might be dull, tedious and pointless but...

"It is! And it's getting bigger!" yells Almona at volume 12. She's from a war zone and is not easily fazed.

The class gawp at the sky.

"We need to ask ourselves why Macbeth has 'murdered sleep'," I say uselessly.

The whole class has now lurched towards the windows in a pantomime of mighty dread.

"It is, though!. It is coming our way!"

'What is?

"A plane Sir!"

Of course it is. We're in West London. Near Heathrow. The plane is landing. It is a mere quotidian occurrence.

They are having a laugh. A cheap laugh. Or not. I pick up some of the panic. Yes, there is something in the sky. A big plane hovers. It might just be a bit louder and lower and closer than usual. And getting bigger all the time.

"We surely need to ask ourselves ..."

What? What? If we're all going to be blown to smithereens!

Bang goes the lesson. SATs is dull enough without having to compete with terrorist interventions.

I attempt a little levity.

"Is it one of ours?"

The class are bemused.

Or is it a bird? Or is it the twister? Or the four horsemen of the apocalypse? What's the drill? My mother always hid us under the table when the Doodlebugs fell. Shall I get them under the desks?

Teaching in London – as Tim Brighouse has recently remarked – is tough enough without all this. Now my pupils live with The Dread – of gas and poison and fire and dirty bombs and tubes that fall off the line and now planes that fall out of the sky. No wonder they're more than usually bonkers. Maybe they aren't just having a lark.

The plane disappears. I lament their cheap histrionics and do some patrician gravitas. We return to our desks.

"Now, where were we?"

"Blood will have blood they say."

A helicopter hoves into view. It rumbles and clatters loudly. A little too loudly. Bang goes Macbeth.

"Don't you worry – it's only Ofsted on a recce! They're in next week. It's me they're after."

Staying behind after class

Published 18 September 2003

I blame Channel 4's *That'll Teach 'Em*. I've gone all 1950s grammar school. My role models are my old teachers. It's been all Gravitas and Grim Visage and No Smiles 'til Christmas.

The merest peccadillo and it's detention. Friday 3.30pm sharp!

And here they are sitting severally and sullenly before me.

Attila Dervish – for putting gum in Jiri's hair. Excised by nurse. Jiri still has bald spot. Dervish still finds it funny.

Decibelle – for histrionics. She was invaded by bees and left the room clutching tresses at volume 11.

Sabrina – for unkindness. Dennis Plum offered to read out loud. I don't know why. Plum reads at about a syllable an hour. It's murder. But there was no need for Sabrina to tell us so.

"Jesus, Sir. Put him out of his misery. For all our sakes."

Jack Shepherd – for no homework again.

"Couldn't do it, Sir – what with all the fightin' and the dogs."

Rhapsody Bland – for being absent.

"The bus blew up on Hammersmith Bridge."

And Charlie Nerk – for being present. For hats, hoods, headphones, gum and probably class As. And because I felt like it.

All the usual suspects. I do some marking and tutting. I try to be as hatchet faced as Sir Alex glaring at a defensive error or Beckham's pony tail. I drone on about standards and discipline and Roman virtues. Woeful drivel.

I try to keep a straight face.

None of us are listening.

The silence is broken. Fresh-faced tots start talking to jaded hooligans. They listen. They talk back. No one's roaring or zooming around the room. This is real conversation. I drop Mr. 50s Grim Visage. I ask real questions.

Decibelle saw something on a ghost train when she was a baby and never got over it. Screaming makes her feel better. Jack's father's in jail and he has to look after his baby brothers and the Rottweilers while his mum works nights.

Attila goes bonkers when the Ritalin wears off.

And Plum might be slow with a book but he's quick with a ball. He's just had trials for QPR. We need a striker. Maybe he's the new Rooney.

And Charlie?

"You don't want to know, Sir." He has the shakes.

I do want to know. But there's no time. The class is too big. The curriculum's too big. And we're all too busy not meeting targets.

Detention is meant to be punitive but we all seem to be having a good time. This is more like some form of rehab. A tea party for Hooligans Anonymous. It's much better than a proper lesson. Maybe I should just do detentions.

Time's up.

"Off you go, then!"

They're in no hurry. They straggle out.

"Same time next week then, Sir."

The fright of the bumble bee

Published 25 September 2003

Four weeks in and my reign of terror continues. The class is purring along nicely. Most are on message. I feel smug.

I am having a plenary.

Then I see one of them!

They're early this year. It's all that global warming.

They're out there. They lurk and hover and bang into windows. The very worst. Worse than fire alarms, gang wars, bonkers fathers, line managers – or Dervish when the Ritalin wears off.

It's still out there!

The class have not seen it.

It goes. Phew! Buzz off. I plough on. It comes back. I bang on.

"What, finally, is the use of the colon ..."

"Aargh! Aargh!" yells Decibelle.

He has struck. He is among us. Pandemonium on wings.

Girls scream and act like helicopters. Decibelle shreds hair. Sabrina goes bats.

Boys go macho and whack the weeny interloper with fists, hats and novels. Mr Wasp has a most deleterious effect on Dervish who flails his personal targets at the whizzing little fellow.

"Shut it!"

Charlie whacks it to a pulp. There's blood upon the board.

There's a lull. We retire to our seats.

I mock their specious histrionics. I stress that in 30 years I have never seen one pupil stung by a wasp.

"It simply doesn't happen!"

I scoff at them.

Silence. I resume the plenary.

"What, finally, is the ..."

"Aargh! Aargh!"

Bedlam. A second piece of havoc flies in. Mr Wasp's brother has come for vengeance. He is whizzing towards me like a Charlie Parker solo.

I will be cool. Watch me! With the reflexes of Thierry Henry I catch it and kill it and flick it away – all in one movement. Va va voom!

Rhapsody goes pallid. So do I – with extreme pain.

It wasn't a wasp. It was a bee. A jumbo bee. A prime, plump and poisonous fellow. My eyes water. My hand puffs up.

The class are riveted with callous fascination.

"I bet that hurts, Sir."

It does. Like piranhas.

"No no – I'm fine," I whimper.

I am saved by the pips. I take my pregnant hand to the school nurse. She sucks out mortal poisons. I am carted off to casualty and get shots for mortal wounds. I must come back – if alive – at Christmas.

I just thought a fine gesture would restore order.

There's nothing you can do about a wasp in the classroom. And even less about a bee. Acts of God before which all classroom skills are as nought.

Still, with any luck, invasions should cease by half term.

Speaking another language

Published 18 March 2004

I leave a dreary twilight workshop for teachers about teaching poetry. I walk past the hall. There's a huge racket from within. I'd forgotten, it's open mike nite. I walk in.

BOOM BOOM! BLAM BLAM! Bass notes run like bone conduction. My last few hairs and fillings may fall out. Sounds howl and crunch like planes crashing. I seem to have trespassed into another world. Another language.

It's packed with the school's more illustrious scoundrels – those hooded wanderers of the corridors. Some work the decks. Some rap over the booming beats.

They've got just 60 seconds. Year 7 tinies to year 11 hoodlums. They've got sharp cartoon aliases and talk in tongues. The audience go bonkers to the rhythm and rhyme and the verbals. To poetry. You don't get examined in this sort of thing.

Poetry isn't dead. Not this kind.

It lives on in my lovely eleventh year. It zooms round their skulls like demon wasps. I must tear off their headphones. I must banish Missy Elliot and Dizzee Rascal and Dr Dre. Who they?

And those mobiles. I must stop that wretched texting – all that clever language. We're here to do proper poetry. Written stuff. The Greats. They didn't have open mike nites.

It was never like this in the 1590s …

"Alright! Hold Tight! It's The Mettafissikal Rap Night! A dog Fight! Between Johnny 'The Blasphemer' Donne and Andy 'Mr Marvellous' Marvell".

Or in the 1790s …

"Yo! It's The Romantik Rap! Between 'Club Foot' Byron and Sam 'the Opium Man' Coleridge. You got 60 seconds!"

My money's on 'Club Foot' … It would have been fun …

But we're not here to enjoy it. We're here to analyse it. We must revise a Carol Ann Duffy poem. We've only done it a billion times. I ponder a rap version. I sound like Charles Laughton with a hernia. It's a most disturbing poem about a schoolboy who goes psycho because poetry was "in another language".

Class doze.

"He'll kill the cat and budgie and us with a breadknife!"

Class doze.

"Cos he can't get enough attention!" I roar. Class gives no attention.

"So he dials the radio!"

"Yo, Sir! The bre' makes a phonecall!" yells Charlie.

"No one wants his autograph!"

"Yo! That's right! Bre' wants an autograph!" Charlie is in italics.

"Sorry?"

"It's Stan Sir!"

"What is?"

"This Duff, Sir! It's Stan! It's an Eminem song!" Charlie then makes brilliant connections between Mr Eminem's song and "that Duff one".

He's in another language. I check out my daughter's CDs. I find Stan. Most disturbing. Just like "that Duff one".

Who wants to read?

Published 30 September 2004

"Who wants to read? Who wants a part?" I ask my lovely not-top 10th year. Hands wave like a reception class.

"Yeah me, Sir! Yeah me!' We're knee deep in our drama module: *A View From the Bridge*. I dish out parts to Silvana, Sabrina, Decibelle, Chubb – and Dennis Plum. The rest throw tiny tantrums.

"I will take the main part."

"What again, Sir?"

"I will be Eddie Carbone."

I've honed this role down over 30 years. Early versions were in the Brando/Pacino tradition. This morning's will be more nuanced, more in the James Gandolfini/Tony Soprano mode.

"Some people would pay to hear this!"

"You wish, Sir!" says Decibelle flicking through the pages. "Wooay! I'm not in it 'til page 16."

I'm in role and in the streets of Little Italy.

"Why's he talking funny?"

"Is it set in Wales, Sir?"

I crank up the menace and threat.

"It weren't me!" says Dillywig who has not realised we're doing a play. Decibelle stares at page 16.

Then it's Sabrina's turn. She plays Eddie's daughter in pure Shepherd's Bush – with added commentary. "I wouldn't put up with that!"

Then it's Silvana's turn as the Italian mother. Silvana was born in Italy. She can't read English. No matter. She trills in a heavenly manner. The class are enchanted – even Furnace, who stops texting. Decibelle rehearses page 16. We're going well.

Then comes Plum. Plum is enacting a lawyer. Plum combines indomitable enthusiasm with functional illiteracy. His first speech is a page long. He coughs and puts a digit on the page.

"Go on my son!" yells Furnace. Plum goes on. He plods on through polysyllables like he's swallowing marbles. Class maintain a generous silence. We've been here before.

Mumble mumble. Class get restless. Decibelle mimes page 16 like a goldfish.

Mumble mumble. Each word is like pulling teeth. Why does he offer to read? Mumble mumble. Dennis still has 23 more lines to go.

We are losing the will to live. Silvana back on lipgloss. Furnace back on texting. Decibelle still on page 16. But reading is good for Dennis' confidence.

"He's rubbish, Sir!"

"Jesus, Sir! Put him out of his misery!"

"And us, Sir! We'll be here 'til Christmas!" I cut Plum.

"Thank you Dennis!" Plum crushed. Plum stops. But I am angry with the class response.

"Manners are worth more than literacy!" I yell. "And so is enthusiasm!"

Dillywig looks for my words in the text. Pips go. Decibelle doesn't. She's still on page 16.

"I just wanted to read, Sir!"

Doing a few lines

Published 25 November 2004

We must line up our classes in the corridor before they enter the room. It supposedly promotes calm and order. Not for me at the moment. My new classroom is a secret dark cell at the end of a corridor which is tiny and tenebrous and echoes like Sun Studios. An arena for mayhem.

Still, I must line them up.

I wait outside my room in Westblock for my not-top ninth year to emerge from the east block. It is the last lesson of the day. They are late. Not entirely their fault. It's a long haul and some forget who I am and where the room might be.

I wait some more. Ah, here come my model pupils Anna and Samantha with satchels full of learning.

"Sorry we're late!" they trill. Sometimes I wish I could do the lesson with just them. But we must wait in a line. I prepare my ruthless stare. Here come some more.

"You're late!" I roar into the echoing murk. They stagger through an unhinged door clouting each other with sacks full of fizzy things and mobiles and Playstations.

"Get in line! Alphabetically!"

This is a bit advanced for some. Many relish the darkness and do fake fights and ghost noises and push and shove and cuss their mums and fall over until our line looks like a train wreck.

"I can't see my head!"

"Look there's a bat!"

"Trick or treat!"

"I am the anti-Christ!"

"You will line up!"

But they can't. There's not enough wall. They must queue both sides. Two train wrecks.

At last there is calm and order. Then I make a big mistake. I wait for those oafs still in transit. The usual suspects. The concave visages of

Dillywig and Decibelle surface. And then the chubby forms of Plum and Furnace and Khaled.

"Why are you so late?"

Playing footie or eating pies or applying lipgloss or just losing the way. Plum thought he had another teacher.

"That fit one sir!"

Khaled just conked out.

"Fasting, sir."

"Me too!" says the heathen Dillywig.

We're finally all lined up.

No, we're not. Magdalena emerges through the crepuscular shades. She is late because she was late for her last lesson and had to wait for a late slip. She apologises in Romany. She is from Prague and is seeking asylum.

We finally achieve a trappist silence. Two perfect lines. You can hear a pin drop. And Dillywig. He has fallen over Plum who has fallen over a football. Decibelle thinks it's funny. It is. Very.

"It's not funny!" I growl. I put the last late wandering oinks – except for Magdalena – in detention.

"Line up! Enter!"

They enter the hushed cell of my classroom for the remaining 17 seconds of the lesson.

Off task and off syllabus

Published 20 January 2005

I'm with my lovely key skills sixth form. The syllabus is dull. The class are bright – a common occurrence. We must look at dismal questions on dismal texts and tick boxes with the least daft answers.

I feel bad. They feel bored. And bewildered. Most pupils have little English and the rest are Ned Crumlin and Albert Plum.

Some are from war zones and terrors and famines. They are seeking asylum – not answers to these witless interrogations. They fecklessly tick the boxes. This is the opposite of education. We drudge on to the 'Fact and Opinion' section. We must spot the difference. I furnish them with an example.

"QPR are the best team in London!"

"Fact!" says Albert. He is a hardcore fan – or a hardcore dimwit.

"Bollocks!" opines Ned. This Socratic dialogue is lost on Yasmin and Magdalena. I must perk things up. Let's try the exam board video on the topic. I press play.

"Warner Brothers" it says.

"Bitesize" it should say.

"The Matrix" it says.

"Strategies for Non Fiction" it should say.

"Yes! Yes!" they chirp perkily. It's the wrong tape.

"Leave it on sir!" Erm

"Go on – it's boom sir!" It might well be boom, Albert, but it's outside the strict parameters of our syllabus.

"Oh go on!" says Ned.

"Please!" says Mercedes.

"No!" We'll be off task. Off syllabus. We're not here to enjoy ourselves

But maybe it's about time we did. Doesn't Barthes talk about the pleasure of the text? He calls it 'jouissance'.

"Oh alright then!"

"Yes! You're cool, Sir."

I turn the lights out and we're off – lost in cyberspace. Perfectly formed bodies zoom about in lurex and leather and shades. They look cool and talk deep. I feel pedagogically guilty. I feel compelled to dissect all this jouissance. I freeze frame it.

"Shall we look at this closer?" I drone quizzically.

"No!" yells Plum – obviously a Barthesian. "Just press play you muppet!"

I do. For the next two lessons. The film holds them spellbound. I think it flash and meretricious. It certainly reaches those parts that those dismal tick boxes don't.

The film ends. We have our best lesson ever. We discuss – in various languages – alternate realities and parallel worlds and fascism and philosophy and Orwell and modes of control.

"The national curriculum might be *The Matrix*, Sir!"

Crikey! But we're off task and target. And I haven't measured any learning outcomes.

"Can I bring in *American Pie* next week sir?" says Mercedes.

"Er, probably not!"

More than my job's worth. We mustn't go off that syllabus.

Running for cover (music)

Published 13 October 2005

I'm having a good day – cruising at Ofsted level 2 towards a free period. Then, whoops! I get a cover slip. Last lesson. Music with the eighth year. The short straw.

I walk in. The room's a racket. The class cheers. I am deemed a soft touch. I survey the scene hatchet-faced. Instruments all over the place. They are a rich repertoire for riot. Clots hit xylophones. Oinks bash drums. There's a buffoon with a bassoon. Pandemonium.

They make The Unteachables look like Malory Towers. They've already given Miss Blossom the cellist shingles.

I don't know their names – except for Dillywig over there. He is jumping on a piano with his bottom, rather in the Little Richard mode. I ask him to desist.

"Too many bum notes." The class might have laughed if they'd heard me. I do a bit of yelling and more hatchet face. They sit down and shut up. Peace. All I want is a little dozing quietude while I invent some retrospective action plans.

I look for register. There isn't one. I hand out blank sheet.

I look for a cover lesson. There isn't one – just some gibberish phoned in by the traumatised Ms Blossom.

"Mozart and Marley Worksheet," it says. It's multiple choice. You know the one.

Did Mozart play the fiddle, the fool, left back – or the harpsichord? Or not.

I give it out. They settle.

Boing! Boing!

Dillywig is now under the piano. He flails at the keys. I slam it shut but fail to break his digits. I lock it up. I kick him out.

There is silence.

"If you've finished, write all you know about Mozart or Marley."

Or point at your head. Or stand on it. Or go to sleep. Just shut up.

We settle. Silence.

Then a very tiny boy gets stuck in a flugelhorn. It makes odd noises. It sound like a squashed dog. This elicits mirth.

"This is not remotely amusing," I drone. It is, I'm afraid, extremely hilarious. I cannot stifle laughter.

I abandon lesson. I tell them I saw Bob Marley at the Coliseum in 1975.

"Whatever!"

I tell them I met Mozart in the streets of Prague in 1742.

"Yeah – whatever!"

Cordelia Swansong smiles and shakes her head. She offers to play the piano. I unlock it. She trills a rather moving version of The Moonlight Sonata. The class are spellbound. Savage beasts are soothed. We ask for an encore.

I collect worksheets. I collect in register. I check list.

Michael Mouse, Donald Duck, Wayne Rooney, Mooch aka Dread and Spiderman have, apparently, been in attendance.

Reading from page 29

Published 9 March 2006

Research has shown that a teacher may have 1,000 or more exchanges with pupils in a single day. That's about a million "transactions" every 5 years. Ergo I must be on about seven million. Scary stuff.

They never told me these things on the PGCE course. I would have stuck to the train driving. Most of my classes are sanctuaries of Socratic dialogue. Well, apart from those grim sessions with Ritalin 8 where transactions tend to implode and multiply. I become Joyce Grenfell with Tourette's.

"Good morning! Right! Just settle down! Right! Aims and objects! Please sit down! Right! Noun clusters! On a chair – good.

"Finbar, hat! What religion? Right! Geena, lipstick! Life's not fair!

"Tell your mother then! Please turn to page 29 of Abomination.

"Stop eatingchewingtalkingtexting Right! No! Share then Page 29! Dilly! Head phones! What? Right! We're not here to 29! Last time. Right!

I must have said "right" a billion times. Is it a transaction?

Rhapsody glazes over. Reads Zadie Smith.

"Right! Attila put him down ... not in the bin! Turn round! Good. What? 29! Right! That's it! I'm going to count to 10."

Shkelzen quite baffled. Is this a maths lesson?

"Perfect!" Silence. Knock! Knock! Enter Ronald Crumlin.

"Sorry, Sir Train Bench on the line."

"Whatever sit note? I do care but we're doing SATs. Just shut it! Right? I am allowed to say shut it. Shut it! Report me Twenty bleedin' nine! On the board! I can say that!

"Yes Shkelzen? 29! Right. Get out of the cupboard Shaka! Twenty bleedin' nine. Right. Any offers to read? Thank you Cordelia."

She purrs fluently down the page. Crash! Crumlin falls off chair.

"Right! That's it! Detention! Carry on Lipstick Geena! Habiba! Knitting! You won't die. Ronald! Thank you. Right. I care not a fig the last time Hat! If What? Why? Right! Offers to read? Thank you Finbar 29!"

"Jesus, Sir he can't!" True. He's on the wrong page. He mumbles and conks out. Knock! Knock! Enter Miss Limpet the Freudian. She prises Shaka out of cupboard and into inclusion unit.

"He mad, Sir!" This is no way for an adult to earn a crust. Dennis Plum has his hand up.

"Yes Dennis?" "Where are we Sir?"

Hell, Dennis! The 29th circle of hell where billions of sentences go to die.

Seth in the sixth form

Published 28 September 2006

The 12th year saunter into my classroom. Other-worldly intellectuals. Like the floppy-fringed Seth. My year 8 saunter out. Worldly-wise street kids. Like the crop-skulled Mooch. He regards the sixth formers with dismay. With their daft hair and grim pallor and skinny cryptic T-shirts. He doesn't realise that they're aesthetes. Deep. Poseurs.

"Wankers!" mutters Mooch.

Mooch belongs to that fierce English tradition of thuggish philistines. Seth belongs to that fine English tradition of languid bohemians – found in sixth forms and universities throughout the land. If you can't fop around in the sixth form when can you? I did. I was a poseur. I blame Bob Dylan. I saw him at the Albert Hall in 1966. The coolest thing on the planet. I soon had the Kerouac hat and existential shades and wrote appalling verse. My English teacher endured this with much patience. It was easier to be a bohemian in those days. Not any more. Seth and his tribe are an endangered species. These days the sixth form is all about modules and targets and uniforms – and you must sign contracts!

"I will be a good boy and wear proper trousers and swot ferociously and participate appropriately."

Or you're out. Expelled.

This is quite beyond Seth. He gets caught drinking vodka and "worse" in the sixth form gardens. He bunks my PSHE class – I wish I could! He plays gigs in dungeons down in Ladbroke Grove. They sound like an air crash. "It's hardcore emo sir!" Whatever that is.

He recites appalling verse. Flocks of girls swoon. He keeps breaking the rules. The contract. He'll get expelled. I must save him. I summon him and his mother. She's a ringer for Patti Smith.

"It's all bollocks this isn't it?" she says. Well, yes. But this is a school and I'm a schoolteacher.

"Just behave yourself!" I plead. We shake hands. "Thank you!"

Things improve. He nearly wears a uniform. He does essays. He attends my PSHE lectures. He makes a real effort during an observed lesson. He is quite scintillating. The lesson ends. Seth comes up to our visitor – another severe consultant.

"He's the best fucking teacher I've ever had!" I smile wanly. The consultant does not. I try to disown the clot.

Kieran now has a haircut like a hedgehog. Jarvis wears kohl and skull earrings and Rhapsody has gone Left Bank and discovered Francoise Hardy. They're bright and funny – and seventeen. A delight. The best. If we continue to treat them like this, we will lose them.

The English girls

Published 26 October 2006

The film of *The History Boys* is terrific. Dazzling, moving, funny and worth umpteen PowerPoint briefings from management gurus. At last! Something about education which doesn't make you lose the will to live. It deals brilliantly with all the big issues. One of them is the "cult of cleverness". And clever boys.

I was an Oxbridge boy – in a posh grammar school in the mid-sixties. We were primped and groomed till we squeaked with the requisite bollocks.

"Lawrence explores subconscious sex drives with compelling insight!" squeaked Titch Perkins.

"Sex for Baudelaire is always, I feel, 'le petit mort'," trilled the moon-faced Dredge. Normal boys were chasing girls and listening to Gene Vincent down at Mac's cafe. We were chasing high culture. Titch and I were dragged into art houses to see the films of Michelangelo Antonioni. "Searing excavations of contemporary sexual ennui" we concluded – virgins barely out of shorts. This tosh was encouraged. Callow, specious, cleverness – as peddled by Bennett's slick Irwin. It got you in.

We were now ready for the Oxbridge interviews.

I blew Cambridge. I just stuttered and Kingsley Amis pronounced me a half-wit.

The Oxford exam was next. The head locked us in his study. I had some rather pert opinions about orgasms in Lawrence. The head forgot we were there. We scribbled way past time. I got in. They probably weighed it. Titch didn't. He'd had some pretty damn clever opinions about Michelangelo Antonioni. Wrong bloke. The question concerned the Renaissance fellow.

Titch was too clever by half.

My sixth form pupils are so much more mature. So much wiser. Their voices and opinions are their own. They listen to each other. It's so much better. Why? Inner city suss? Perhaps. Varied backgrounds? Perhaps. Above all, it's because there's GIRLS in the class. Tough, wise, sharp west London girls. Not baying posh home counties boys. Girls stifle pretension and clobber clever dicks. Titch and I would be deemed tossers.

They have a most benign effect on Seth and his chums. They mix high and low culture. John Donne and Lily Allen. John Webster and PJ Harvey. They have humility. Despite all those silly targets I can try to teach more like Bennett's Hector. They may not be Oxbridge bound but there's no dumbing down. They're nicer, brighter than we ever were. They're not victims of the "cult of cleverness".

Those History Boys need my English Girls.

Know what I'm sayin' sir

Published 26 April 2007
"Wag 1! Wigwam!" says the scamp Dillywig at me. He breezes into my class with off message, off buttock trousers and offers a tribal handshake.

"Wag 1 sir!" I wave a non-tribal hand. "Wag 1, sir!" We do knuckles. Welcome to Planet West London. I need a glossary. I consult my 12th intellectuals for translations and transcription (see below).

We're having a tutor-set dawn workshop. They're meant to be swotting like billyho. They're not. They're just chilling. I must perk them up.

"Success comes from hard work, not luck." "As if."

"Oh, sir lowit!" trills Dills. He joins his chums for some deep wordage.

"There's beef, blad." Eh? "There was this bredrin' innit and he got shanked with a shank, he got shanked in the back and there was blood everywhere innit, it was off – key! Know what I'm sayin' blad!"

Subtitles please! It's enough to give that Lynne Truss kittens. But I like it. I'd give it an A. Fat chance! Wrong code. Wrong class. It's vibrant and sharp and it communicates. Much more than those AQA speaking and listening exemplar tapes.

Decibelle breezes in. Late. "Sorry sir I just got cherpsed by this boy!" Eh? She joins her chums. "I swear down Miss Coles is safe, know what I'm sayin' sir?" Of course I don't. I'm not meant to. I'm on another planet. Planet Teacher. The land of "edu babble". Where language goes to die. Where we must attend "learning area twilight workshops" delivered by PowerPoint in high gibberish.

We sit and stifle mirth while consultants twitter about the latest daft wheezes. Homework is now "independent learning and research tasks". My lessons are "learning cycles" in four movements (connection, activation, demonstration and consolidation). What larks!

We hear about "the nine gateways of personalised learning" and "ownership of the school's vision". These clots would fail any GCSE speaking and listening exam. They can't speak and they're not listening. It's unspeak. Dull, dead and patronising.

We hear of "positive failure policies!" Crumlin and Lunk have been big on these since year 7! This is moronic. Well, oxymoronic. Beyond satire. "Tragic patois," says the head of King Edward VI at an anti-edubabble conference. We all agree. "Lowit, Mr PowerPoint! Know what I'm sayin'?"

NB: Wag 1! - an expression of warm greetings, derived from "what's going on?" You're on your own with the rest...

Weapons of class disruption

Published 14 June 2007

Many years ago we had a talk from a head of a high school in New York City – about inner city violence and weapons of destruction. The "Other America".

"It's the 12 year olds who scare me!" he said. Crikey.

"They can't shoot straight!" Crumbs.

"It's coming your way. Weapons. Same culture!"

Well, it seems it just might have done. Tabloids seem to think so. We hear of knives and guns. We've been empowered to search for them.

That should do it.

It might go thus – 10th year English trudge in of a morning.

I put fingers in flak jacket and strafe mites with the zero tolerance gaze. I stop at the usual suspects. Lunk and Furnace.

"Good morning!" I trill.

"Might be!" grunts Lunk. They're rather knackered what with the pillage and gang wars down Ladbroke Grove.

"Hands up if you're carrying a knife!" "Big Ant" Furnace raises tattooed limb.

"Anthony! This isn't good enough!" "Fair cop, sir!"

He puts a dagger in our Amnesty box.

"Sorry, sir! I am most remiss!"

"Next!"

I look at Lunk. He looks leery. I give him a body search. He does not kill me. I find blade. I bin it.

"But why oh why Sidney?"

"It's that peer group pressure sir. A malign subculture! It has quite done for me, sir!"

I look daggers at Shaka. He threads his dreads and negotiates a deep skunk haze.

"I hope you're not succumbing to lazy stereotypes here, sir!" Fair cop.

"Check Rhapsody, man – she tooled up!"

Rhapsody puts down her Zadie Smith – and bins a Bowie knife.

"Sir, this is utterly tedious. Can you please teach me something! I'm trying to get into Oxbridge, here!"

We proceed with the lesson. As if.

I'm not Roboteacher and they're not gangstas.

Of course knives are a grave problem but, thank goodness, it's still very rare. I have never seen a knife in 30 years of inner city teaching.

The recent hysteria helps no one.

Check out *The Wire* instead. The best TV programme ever. Up there with Dickens. Written by a former cop and teacher, it explores that "Other America" with intelligence and compassion. That war between street and school. No preaching. No glib answers. And yes, some of that culture is coming our way.

"Right class! Where were we?"

"Macbeth, sir."

Ah yes. Carry on Rhapsody!'

"Is this a dagger I see before me?"

For whom the bell pips

Published 12 July 2007

These final weeks are tough going. I wander maudlin down corridors. I keep almost blubbing. It's saying goodbye to the leavers that does for me.

Like most of my 11th year.

I can still see them on their first day under the big oak tree in the north playground. All lined up and shining in the dappled light of the September sun. And now I see them on their last day sitting in the falling light of our classroom. Five years have passed. 1,500 hours. All gone in a blink. My merry crew all gone.

No more Stanley Plum? Solid, decent Plum. A teenage Horatio. Whither Plum? No more Lily Rose? Sunny, laughing Lily. My register monitor. Whither Lil? And no more Dave Mania! Crazy, bonkers Dave. The Pimpernel of the West Block. I've so often wished him gone and now I want even him to stay. He's always been off target, message, chair, stream, trolley and rocker. He's rather been on feet, heat, drugs, corridors and a hiding to nothing. I've tried to be his teacher and tutor – and once his character witness. He was up for burgling a house. I did my best. But the case collapsed. It was my house. He'd nicked half my record collection. Even Blonde on Blonde. That's a triple Asbo. He's since gone "straight". Ho hum. Whither Dave?

We all reminisce. There's much cheering and clapping and waving of shaving cream and scrawling of farewells on cards and T-shirts and tummies. What a rich mix of children! They've always taken care of each other. They've always been generous and tough and funny. London's finest. And they're all still here and they've done all right.

I feel compelled to give a valediction.

I tell them they're all wonderful and it's been a privilege to be with them. Even Mania. "Easy, sir!" I try to dredge up some final invincible wisdom.

"Kindness trumps everything!"

"Is that it?" Well, yes. It is.

They play some music. Some even dance. Vladimir with Lily and Plum with Rebecca and is that Mania getting down with Lucy? Then they play *Stand by me* and I'm quite done for. Almost blubbing.

Dave shuffles over to shake my hand.

"You're alright, considering." Considering I'm a naïve clot.

Rachel gives me a rose nicked from the sixth form gardens.

Pip! Pip! Pip! The final pips! Ask not for whom they pip.

They pip for you!

"Goodbye! Good luck! Off you go!"

I watch them dawdle past that big oak tree and disappear through the school gates forever into the unkind world.

Send for Roland

Published 20 September 2007

The year begins to settle. Most classes purr along nicely. Except for the not-top 8th year. They keep me out of the comfort zone – and into the white-knuckled zone. Dull it isn't. Stupid they're not. 'Low ability'? they're not – that's just an alibi for indifference. This is where the lost and luckless go. Where the damaged get disappeared. They're gifted and talented in the wrong literacies and languages. They get frustrated and antic. Or maybe it's those E numbers making them fizz. Whatever. Mr Cameron wants them back in a dunce's hat in primary school.

We're discussing Robert Swindell's *Abomination*. We're having a shrieking and not listening lesson. Level 7. Some just doze and some frolic as floridly as any on Big Brother. There's Kaline who prompts migraine and makes that Charlie seem an elected mute. There's Nexhimje from

Tirana who is an elected mute and seeks asylum. There's Tuvshin from the Grove who's an elected clot who's got his hair caught in a fan and there's Sissy from a tugboat on the Thames who mutters monologues about Mr Donut and there's Phoebe from the Embassy who reads Pushkin and Finbar from King Hell Mansions who's lost the plot and Ms Limpet from the Partially Stupid Unit ministering to his infant mind. 'She mad!' All those little lives.

I've made all the right moves. I've done all that behaviour modification workshop stuff. I've done boundaries and limits. Savage gravitas and no smiling 'til Christmas. High expectations and zero tolerance. Seating plans and hand ups. And never talking until there's silence! We'll be here til Guy Fawkes... All the gubbins. It doesn't take.

I chalk an arrow and the word teacher and stand under it.

I need help. They need help. Time for Roland! Who he? My chum from inclusion. He comes in like a Zen master and all is calm. His heart beats once an hour. Roland knows. He knows what they're up to. He knows what I'm up to. A rare gift. He can scare them silly but he's on their side.

"He the man!?" says Finbar. He's got that charisma. Can I have some? It's not so easy when you're a permanent and quotidian fixture.

We return to our novel. We have a sprightly discussion. They see that I might teach them something. When Roland leaves we still purr along nicely. Maybe I need a replica of Roland in the room? A virtual version? Spreading that Zen calm. Meanwhile it's back to plan B. I'll have to wear them out with ruthless empathy. It might well take all year.

Any nonsense and we'll send for Roland.

Shut the **** up!

Published 5 February 2009

Have you ever sworn in the classroom? Of course not! It's very Bad Practice. I did. Once. In 30 years. It went thus...

It's the last lesson of a wretched winter's afternoon. I'm with the Not Top 8th year. I'm knackered and migrained. I take the register. I get to Sidney Mayhem. Wind Up Artiste Supreme. I call his name.

"It weren't me," he yells satirically.

We proceed. We're reading *Stone Cold* by Robert Swindell. The class love it. Throughout Sidney mutters. We stop. We start. He starts again.

"Please be quiet."

"You're picking on me! You're racist!" Eh?

"Cos I'm Irish!" Eh?

We continue. So does Sidney.

"Be quiet!"

There's a lull. We resume. Crash! He slides down the wall off his chair. He solicits moron approval. We proceed. Now he's flaunting headphones and grunting along to that Eminem fellow. I confiscate them and send him out of the room. He does baboon impressions through a window. My migraine blooms. We have silence for 10 minutes. Then I smell burning. Sidney waves paper at me. It is on fire. I calmly stop this. I put it out. I wish I could put him out. I suggest, calmly, that he is a "dickhead"!

"You can't say that!" He's right. I can't. We crawl towards the end of the lesson. Sidney mutters like a drill on open nerves.

"Right!" I glare at Sidney. I pause. I attempt the full Roy Keane stare. And a big Pinter pause. "Yes, sir?" This is war.

"Just shut the fuck up!"

I relish each loud, flat, monosyllable. So do my pupils. Some clap. Some flick thumb and forefinger. A hush falls. We finish the chapter. I dismiss class. I keep Sidney behind. I cart him off to Mr Heavy, the deputy head.

"Sir, he swore at me! A teacher," bleats Sidney. "Called me a dickhead!"

Mr Heavy looks grim. Mr Heavy is old school. I delineate Sidney's various sins and pyromaniac tendencies. Mr Heavy looks grimmer. He eyeballs Sidney – with savage proximity.

"Do you know why?" he thunders. He relishes the moment.

"Because you are a fucking dickhead!" Sidney goes pale.

"Do that again and I'll take you behind the bike sheds!"

He smiles at me. "Won't we, Mr Whitwham?"

"Well, yes."

I smile thinly. I'm a wet liberal. A sixties hippy. A clot.

Mr Heavy makes some further observations. Sidney's mother might not recognise him. His face might be re-arranged. That area. Appalling stuff. But Sidney never gave me grief again. And I never swore again.

It's very Bad Practice.

Chapter 2

In the mode pedagogic

'He's read more than you can lift!'

I'm a child of the sixties. Bliss was it to be alive in London and bliss would it be to teach especially English. The prince of subjects. Off I went to the Institute of Education – a fabulous island of academe. I was taught by the late great Harold Rosen, Basil Bernstein and James Britain. Serious intellectual heavyweights. We explored language and learning and literature and class. Thrilling stuff. We had lectures from Allen Ginsberg and RD Laing who said that schools drove you 'mad'. Teaching was a dangerous, subversive activity. Fabulous! We would destroy the class system. We could do anything. We were Blake's children. We were the storm troopers of Albion. We were utter clots. Idealistic clots. We charged into classrooms waving Blake and Adrian Mitchell. My goodness we'd make the blighters creative. It was fabulous. Never been better. Or more fun. Or more daft. Classroom management was seldom addressed. Thugs from the den weren't too keen on Gerard Manly Hopkins – or Jimi Hendrix at volume 11. Working class boys deemed us half-wits. The revolution never happened. We were chastened. But I still want to do that stuff. Dull it wasn't.

And how dull it is now. The present pedagogy is pretty thin gruel. English seems to have been shrunk to a branch of business management. Information retrieval. There's little intellectual muscle. Little political suss. Little awareness how language works. We don't teach. We deliver and facilitate. Outcomes must be measured and targets must be met. We teach to the test and zoom up the charts. So it's schemes of work and action plans and workshops with Ms Mumps and her mission statements. She's got us by the modules. So we duck and weave and survive just like the pupils. And ...sshh... you can still smuggle most things into English.

Set texts meet sex txts

Published 29 April 2004

"Licence my roving hands ..." I drone at the sixth form. We seem to be doing a lot of erotica lately. I get paid for this! It's an outrage. Some people have to do quadratics, dovetail joints and bunsen burners. And here I am doing pornography. Someone should be told.

Still, I have no choice. It's a set text. We're doing England's greatest poet John Donne. On His Mistress going To Bed. Some of the class can't resist comparing his work with the greatest living Englishman – and recent British Book Award winner – David Beckham.

Set text with sex txt. With Beckham's recent love lyrics in *The News of The World*. They quote.

"I want to slide my hands up your *******."

Both Donne and Beckham seem to be subverting the petrarchan tradition. The classroom's the wrong place for this stuff. I feel most embarrassed.

Just like I did as a sixth form pupil in my 1950s single-sex grammar school. Spotty callow virgins barely out of shorts, we were suddenly knee deep in French filth.

Then it was orgasm and death in Baudelaire. This gave most of us a turn for the worse. We thought necrophilia was just daft and hopefully outside the experience of most people. Mr Hills, our English teacher, was always sexing things up. Marvell's poetry, for example.

"Luscious Clusters ... stumbling on melons." He loitered around the words with unseemly relish. We just felt embarrassed.

I was much more interested in The Shangri Las and Jerry Lee Lewis than all that poetry. You knew where you were with Great Balls of Fire.

Now I'm the teacher and I'm still embarrassed. More, it appears, than most of my students.

I drone on with Donne ...

"Before, behind, between, above, below."

Joe and Jesse perk up. Oxbridge candidate, Alice, goes deaf. I emphasise the technical brilliance. I attempt a strong post-feminist line. Cordelia laments Donne's misogyny – and my blushing waffle. Even Alice demands a more rigorous exegesis.

"What – exactly – do the words mean?'

"Orgasm! Erection!"

"Oh ..." She blushes like I did at Baudelaire. Cleo and Sofia think that Donne is really hot and discuss Jacobean lingerie in relentless detail.

On I plod.

"I am naked first!"

"Just like Beckham!" says Sofia. She quotes one of his txts.

"When I cu i'll so be in your **** i'll ..."

"Yes ... yes ... thank you!"

I must change the subject.

"Jesse – if Donne was alive today ... what position would he play? Right midfield?"

"Pathetic!" sighs Cordelia.

Sage and mentor

Published 9 September 2004

Most of my chums in the English department left last year. They fled or fell at the chalk face. I am surrounded by neophytes and NQTs. Which leaves me in the role of sage and mentor. Or is it dead wood and bedblocker?

I must be an academic sage and provide the dread schemes of work – at A level.

I thought we had these. Rather impressive tomes plump with the scholarship of my defunct chums. Apparently not. Said chums were fluffy dilettantes. Ofsted wants severe professionals.

I burn midnight oil and concoct bucketloads of lessons all couched in the requisite gibberish. If you need this stuff, you're doomed. I'm with Arsene Wenger at this level. "If you tell a player what to do you kill his creativity."

And I must be practical mentor and provide behaviour management tips.

Any fule kno these. You must plan, prepare, pace, organise, manage and be confident, calm, clear, assertive, assured, consistent, patient, positive, formal, structured, differentiating, firm but fair and have a low voice and high expectations and a seating plan and whizzo body language and an Armani suit and carry out all threats and always talk in jargon and never be their friend and never smile 'til Christmas and have the confidence of Jose Mourinho and the charisma of Johnny Depp.

Easy. Have I missed anything? I go to Waterstones for the latest stuff. There's loads of glum volumes. I pick one. Let's see: *Behaviour Management*. I note three essential moves.

1) "Do not open your mouth until you have complete and total silence and every student is looking at you."

Not half. Although in my experience this may not occur for the first 10 minutes of the lesson or until November – or ever. While waiting I can "knit" or "read a novel". I'd complete a huge woolly or a Russian novel while waiting for the eighth year to attain a tantric silence on a wet Thursday.

2) "Never raise your voice." Absolutely. I've never mastered this. I tend to have blaspheming interior monologues and then go into early Scorcese mode. This merely causes mirth. Scorcese heroes tend not to be four-eyed and balding or from the home counties.

3) "Perfect the deadly stare." I wish. You must look like Dr Lecter or Roy Keane with a number one for this. I look like an owl. This "deadly stare", we learn, involves "a fixed stare and a raised eyebrow and pursed mouth". You try doing this. You just look unhinged. My 10th year would have me sectioned.

I don't relish this sage and mentor role. Still, with a sober suit, a bit of gravitas and some foggy jargon, I might just wing it. As long as they don't visit my lessons.

The fine art of fibbing

Published 9 December 2004

My lessons have lately been enhanced by a lot of lying. I can't seem to stop it. I go from little fibs to the more baroque of porkies. I'm not sure why. Perhaps it's teaching noun clusters or Sats strategies or *Of Mice and Men* for the millionth time – or just the end of term.

But I just carry on fibbing. It has had a generally benign effect on my pupils. Targets are met, results go up and attention is sharper. Except for the ferociously cerebral Rhapsody Bland.

I'm trawling through a rather famous poem with the sixth form. Most of the class doze amiably. Rhapsody doesn't. Her pen waits on my next thrilling insight. We come across a murky passage. They don't get it. Nor do I. The longer I look at it the less sense it makes.

Rhapsody is impatient for explication. I still don't know what it means. I should tell the class this. It's good for them to see an old pedant wrestling with ambiguities. But I don't. I launch into some pompous nonsense.

"Metaphorical resonance ... semantic force field dark nihilism!"

Mumbo jumbo. Most pupils find this more fun than professional competence.

Rhapsody does not.

"What exactly do those words mean, Sir?"

Well, erm, I'll have to ask Dr Barnes, a woman of severe scholarship. I ask Rhapsody to take the wretched text to her.

"Help!" I scrawl below the arcane passage.

Rhapsody leaves. I waffle on. Rhapsody returns waving an exegesis. I open it.

"You are teaching a misprint! Or a typing error. It is 'did' not 'died.' You are a buffoon of the first order!" scribbles the good doctor.

Fair cop. I apologise to class.

I have been hoodwinked by a corrupt text.

Rhapsody has not been hoodwinked by me.

"Dr Barnes says you are a half-wit, Sir!"

"Thank you Rhapsody! Can we please move on to line three."

But this doesn't stop the literary fibbing – especially with any American set text. I claim to have been there and done it. Steinbeck? I was a cowboy in California. Kerouac? I've hitched down highways with cowboy angels.

Ginsberg? Met him! And Southern Gothic? A fibber's heaven. And I've met Professor Longhair in a bordello.

One of these is even true! I'm just sexing up the texts. But Rhapsody still gazes grimly at me. I feel a fraud. I must stop this fibbing.

"There is a Father Christmas!" I say, " And Santa Claus is coming to town! And there'll be peace on earth!"

Happy hols!

Gory details of Macbeth (press rewind)

Published 3 February 2005

We're watching a video. We're knee deep in gore. A figure lurches up some steps. He teeters on the edge.

Swish! Goes a sword. Slice! Goes a blade. Bounce! Goes a head.

"Yo!" go the boys. "Ewww!" go the girls. The head rolls goggle eyed.

"Yo!" The trunk spurts blood. "Yeah!"

What is this? Kill Bill? No! Kill Mac! – Polanski's version. We are studying *Macbeth*. You have to for SATs. Daft. We had enough trouble with *Stig of the Dump*.

"Rewind, Sir! Press rewind!" yells Lunk. He tries to freeze the exact moment of severance. Several times. The class discuss it like Alan Hansen dissecting an offside.

"There!"

"No! It's still on! There!"

Violet has a turn for the worse.

"Is it real, Sir?" she wonders.

She's had quite enough of spurting veins and spouting throats and those grotesque Playboy bunny witches. I press stop. I pontificate. We're not here to watch video nasties. We're meant to be exploring the metaphysics of evil.

I press play. We proceed to the denouement. The dripping head is now on a stick. "Eeerrrr!" yells Violet.

I've always had trouble with drama. It started with those dreaded theatre trips I had as a pupil. 'Chunk' Jones dragged us off to a French classical tragedy – the funniest thing I've ever seen.

What were these Gallic tragedians doing in High Wycombe? There was much heaving and cleavage and snogging and waving of broomsticks – and too few clothes. Then Hector emerged.

A teetering anorexic, his unmuscled limbs were swaddled in dish rags.

"Je suis Hector!' he squeaked. He did a bit of flailing and told us that he would kill anything that moved. In French. Then Rumble fell off his seat. We were snotty with mirth.

Then Chunk stood up. He apologised to Hector, who flounced out. We were dragged out and later hit with sticks.

"You will never go to the theatre again!" he yelled.

Some hope now I'm the teacher taking similar clots on theatre trips. Theatre companies still don't seem to get it. Why do actors look so daft? Why are fights so hopeless? Why was Cleopatra topless?

Schoolboys just get the giggles. Hamlet at the Young Vic was going well until he emerged stark naked from a bath. Why? Even Rhapsody couldn't see how this was aesthetically justified.

"Press rewind!" yells Lunk. The class are now watching the film backwards. They are laughing their heads off – and Macbeth's!

Scooby-dooby Doo

Published 24 March 2005

There's a Zen calm in cell block 101 these days – especially with the ninth SATs class. The Tourettes' Club has become a Quaker meeting. We are bereft of the usual frolics. I'm cruising at top management levels.

You can hear pins drop and mobiles chirrup and fans hum and me drone – about Banquo's ghost or QPR's late push for the play offs. Are they finally paying homage to the sage dotard before them?

No. What has caused this calm? The dread of SATs? No. Ruth Kelly and her zero tolerance? Not at all. What then?

Knitting.

That's what. Many seem to be knitting. They twiddle away with bits of string or plastic. They're making wristbands, headbands, key rings or just nothing. It's called Scoubidou.

It's come back. Knitting is the new rock'n'roll. It's the latest craze. These children of the inner-city, these the tough posses of Ladbroke Grove are knitting. All those other brute distractions and they're knitting!

Has it come to your school yet?

Knit! Knit! Knit! Is there a SATs in it? Are they doing role play for the French Revolution? Crones by the Bastille. Is it therapy? A new religion? Gossips with their rosaries.

Knit! Knit! Knit! It cuts across gender and culture. Ayanna and Yasmin twiddle away.

Decibelle too. She fidgets only with her digits. And look at Furnace! A cartoon of your worst nightmares – an ASBO waiting to happen – he's swapped the attention span of a gnat for the focus of a monk. He too is doing the Scoubidou.

Is this all a wind up?

Knit! Knit! Knit! Should I stop it? Are they merely fiddling while the curriculum burns? No – these crazes soothe them.

We had marbles or transfers or ciggy cards. We drew Gloucester Javelins on Brigitte Bardot or a moustache on Miss Hodgson's grim visage. Keith Goss bought in pet frogs in his pockets. He passed the 11-plus.

My pupils have had Care Bears, goth dolls, punk trolls, mutant skulls and clackers. Yo yos, J Los and Grand Theft Autos. Pokemon, Walkmen, Stick Men and all that green and gungy slime.

Some goth girls had rodents on their persons. Live ones. Rats and mice. They offered solace – and were rather effective teaching aids for *Of Mice and Men.*

This knitting promotes a busy quiescence. Oral work has perked up. Writing too – although it's not always easy to twiddle and scribble. Some teachers use Mozart to achieve this calm. Or feng shui, wind chimes or Ritalin. Horse whispering is, apparently, the next big thing.

But Scoubidou beats the lot. I'd make it compulsory.

Teaching the unteachables

Published 3 November 2005

We're enduring yet another CPD twilight session – successful learning outcomes. I would rather eat my head. We gaze at PowerPoint pictures in glacial rage. Mr Twerp – our shiny, antic "trainer" – trawls the bleedin' obvious. The usual guff floats across the screen.

"Paradigm interface database significant intervention."

This is a virtual world. Quite untethered to my classroom. Mr Twerp never mentions pupils. I wish some of mine would show up. I wish Crumlin and his merry crew would make a significant intervention - come crashing through that screen like the ugly truth.

We move into workshop groups. Mrs Twerp is now our guru. Her theme is "What makes a good plenary?" She too finds the bleedin' obvious thrilling. My plenaries seem to be rubbish. My closing disquisitions are, I'm afraid, often truncated by a mass bolt for the door. Bad practice! She trills on. And on.

We're saved by the pips. No time for a plenary. There's a mass bolt for the door - and the boozer.

I go home and turn on the TV. What's this? Channel 4's *The Unteachables.* Please! No more gurus! But I give it a go. I get dragged in. Philip Beadle is working with some very challenging pupils. They're larking about and writing autobiographies. Tough critters.

They're just like my 10th year. Just like Crumlin and Lunk and Decibelle. This is the real world. At last – a programme that tangles with real issues. It's raw, painful and honest. Philip Beadle clearly likes children. He relishes their dark arts, their wind up wit. He's terrific. Fast and funny – and sometimes, thank goodness, reassuringly useless.

He takes risks. Just like my battered chums used to do so long ago – when teaching was the best job in the world. Before the Twerps and their targets got their chill mitts on us. Before management cowed us. Before Ofsted shrank us.

But wouldn't Mr Beadle fail Ofsted? No starter. Dodgy discipline. Off message. Off trolley. A bit of bad language. And a bit of a laugh. My 10th year would like him. He would inspire them. He inspires me. To teach how I want.

I haven't got long left. Time for a few more larks. Time for that lesson on spontaneous bop prosody. Or the Chinese Whispers novel. Or shall we do that thousand similes lesson?

Look out Ronald Crumlin! Look out my little hooligans! No more measurable outcomes. No more plenaries. No more fear. You won't know what hit you! I'm about to fascinate you – like I used to do.

Cheers Mr Beadle.

Leaving it all for higher education

Published 22 February 2006

Most of the time we superteachers preside over classrooms hushed with contemplation and learning. Teaching, as those pert adverts stress, can be richly rewarding.

Sometimes, however, it can be otherwise. Sometimes after a week of the 8th year and the millionth trawl through *Stig of the Dump* and grocers' plurals and psychotic phonics and the Burger King riot ... it can be the opposite of rewarding.

And Dillywig. And yelling at hoodlums to keep left, quiet, on a chair, in a room and to stop running, stay sitting, remove coats, hoods, gum, phones and bolts. And Dillywig. Sometimes I'd rather be flipping burgers or pruning roses.

Or lecturing at a university. I could have done that.

Some of my lecturers just droned while we snoozed. A sort of Narcoleptics Anonymous. We didn't yell or riot. We didn't use solvents or suggest our mothers were sex workers.

We didn't disturb them and they didn't disturb us. Professor Ward fell asleep and off a lectern during some ruminations on nuns' hairshirts. We didn't notice. The cleaning ladies woke us with broomsticks.

"Think he's done love!"

Robert Graves once gave us a lecture on the White Goddess. To alleviate any tedium attendant on his arcane musings, he brought in a visual aid. His mistress. Gina Lollobrigida. She pouted. He wittered. We gawped at her sumptuous form. Shameless.

Nice work if you can get it.

I bet I could do it. I could do that higher learning. I'd get the beard and lectern and sex up a post-feminist reading of Stig. They'd be rocking in the aisles.

But could they do the learning?

FR Leavis? Terry Eagleton? With the 8th year on a wet Thursday? Doctor Leavis on The Canon and the Grocer's Plural? Professor Eagleton on The Semiotics of Stig? They wouldn't last 2 minutes.

"You're 'avin a laugh!"

"Tell him, Prof! He's cussin' my mum!"

"Jesus! Even Wigwam's better than this!"

They'd be toast. They might have to cart in that Chantelle or that 50 Cent fellow. Otherwise my little scholars would be up the walls and out the windows and back at Burger King. And they'd be down the job centre.

University teachers have got to shape up a bit more these days. They must meet the odd target and have measurable outcomes. I'm better off with the lower learning. I'd miss my merry crew. I'd miss the larks. And I'd even miss even the dread Dillywig.

Never mind the bollocks

Published 2 March 2006

I'm in another twilight workshop. Knee deep. You've been there. You sit round a big table while a consultant murders the English language. The more you listen the less it means.

I nod wanly at each bullet point. I try to construct an earnest listening visage and look like a born again cretin. Will this ever end? Doesn't anyone else want to get back for Arsenal v Real?

Our topic is, apparently, Preparing for Inspection. Why do we never talk about literature any more? I lose the will to live. I get out a book by Ted Wragg. I hide it under a league table.

I read about the lunacy hour. I get the giggles. I read about inspection tips. "Dress as a member of the opposite sex." More giggles. I imagine my tutor group's response. I nearly fall off chair laughing.

I must have "mad curriculum disease – the symptoms of which are an unsteady gait and uncontrolled laughter". I must stop. I think of root canal work and mission statements.

To no avail. I splutter merrily on to the bitter end. Next day I get a note from line management. It harangues me for "inappropriate mirth". I am unprofessional. Newly qualified teachers will find me a poor exemplum.

I blame Ted Wragg. He's been causing me rather appropriate mirth for 30 years. Which is why I had to go to his memorial service last week at the Institute of Education.

I wander past Senate House and my former groves of academe. It was the summer of '67. I see the ghosts of Basil Bernstein and Harold Rosen and James Britton – guiding lights whom I still follow. Passionate. Serious. Funny. Like Ted Wragg. I walk past the blossoms of Russell Square where we decided to change the world. Idealistic clots.

The service is moving and serious and funny. Philip Beadle remembers some key Wragg wisdom. "Bollocks to the bishops!" it went. Professor Brighouse corrects him. It was "absolute bollocks" – as far as he can recall.

This certainly trumps the fashionable "word power wisdom" or anything our consultant might have said. I meet a couple of chums from '67. They're still at it. Bald but burning bright. We laugh at our silly ideals. We laugh even more at modern managementspeak. We wish it would go away.

And I wish Ted Wragg had been at that twilight meeting. He would have winked at us and said: "Bollocks! Bollocks to the bishops!"

A fine exemplum for NQTs.

Meanwhile I must ponder which frock to wear for the next inspection.

It'll soon wear off, sir!

Published 7 September 2006

A crisp summer sun falls across the North playground – and across the new 7th year. Their first day in big school. All scrubbed and togged up, they stand in hushed lines. Nervous parents smile and bonny teachers beam.

The precise light seems to fall on them like a blessing. What a piercing sight! There they are with creaking satchels and brand new bags all stuffed with Potters and Pullmans and pencils and sharpeners and compasses and carrots and buns. Only a few look lost.

I gaze upon the almost prelapsarian scene – upon the little, shining 7th years.

Then I see Dilliwig of my more fallen 10th year. He skulks behind a chestnut tree. He has acquired a skull cut over the hols. He looks daft. He resembles Nosferatu. I hail the hooligan. "Just think! You were like that once Dills! All bright and bushy tailed!" He goes harrumph. "It'll wear off, sir!" he mutters.

I remember him on his first day. He had foppish curls and grey flannels and Startrite shoes and was busy disowning his mother. Now he's got a number one and off-the-buttock baggies and big boots and is busy dissing the system.

What is he doing here?

"My sister, sir! Over there!" He points to an apple-cheeked girl alone in a blade of light. "My little sister!"

Bells ring. Ask not for whom they toll. They toll for your tots. Time for you parents to drift tearful through the gates. Time for your darlings to be carted off to Big School.

I meet 7-7 for English in the afternoon. Our first lesson. I line them up in Trappist silence. I must be fierce. Management are big on this. Tough love. Tight ships, clear boundaries, high expectations. And no smiling 'til Christmas. Get this wrong and you've got bedlam forever. I tell them a story. Pandora's Box. They sit rapt with cherub faces and gobstopper eyes. We have a rather trenchant discussion – fizzing and philosophical and on about level 10.

They're as bright as pins. They leave severally. I clock the brand new Dillywig. A girl thanks me for the lesson and is not deemed a creep. Why can't it always be like this? What happens? Dillywig and Lunk are what happens. They're in detention – for winding up their new Science teacher.

"What? First day!"

"Never done nothing" They seem to have been never doing this for several years.

"He's a donut." I pay the clots no heed. I wax lyrical about my new 7th and his little sister.

"They're fantastic! So much promise!" "It'll soon wear off, sir! You wait and see!"

Telling ghost stories (spooked!)

Published 30 November 2006

Last lesson of the day. The light grows dim. Me too. I totter on towards the end of term. The 7th year totter in. Week 12 module 89 section 9 – Aims and Objectives – enough! enough! Let's flee this dreary treadmill.

"Storytime!" I yell.

"Hurrah!" they yell back.

"It's called 'Harry' – by Rosemary Timperley."

A cracker. Never fails. Any class, any level.

"Not for those of a nervous disposition!" I warn.

Shaka, Ol and Miftar, rendered brutish by "Kung Fu Skull Smasher" and its ilk, do mock fear.

"You say sir!" says Ol.

"It's very scary!"

"Lights outs, then, sir?" Why not? A Trappist hush falls. The classroom grows crepuscular.

"Who wants to read?" Arms zoom up. I love this class. They've got enthusiasm – even the functionally illiterate. I must give them all a turn. Let's go! Max and Lou on level 2 just mumble and conk out. Milhajo is on level 10 – in Croatian – and rather flounders too. Cassandra drones like a shipping forecast and Larry is a five words an hour man.

"Go on my son!" says Ol. But the class's patience runs out.

"Put him out of his misery sir!" "We'll be here 'til Christmas sir!" He could well be right. "You read sir! Do the funny voices! You're good!"

I'm flattered. It's pathetic. Off I go with the tawdry histrionics. I sound like Brian Blessed on speed. They're transfixed. The classroom gets darker. I read on.

"I went to the window to draw the curtain." I go to our window and draw the curtain.

"A long thin clear cut shadow passed..." A long thin rather clear-cut shadow passes our window! Pandemonium.

"Waargh! Waargh!"

"It's a ghost though innit!" yells Ol. A hooded figure passes by in a blizzard of leaves. Its grim visage turns towards us. Even Shaka looks shaky. Me too. Who this? The ghost of Notting Hill? Crumlin's dad come for revenge. Ofsted?

No. Not at all. It's Tommy the caretaker. Hoovering up the autumn leaves. He moves off into the murk. I assure the class it was merely

Tommy. I turn on a light. There is calm. I proceed. I finish the story with its killer ending. Class applaud.

"Just the best, sir! Wicked!"

Shall we now do work on it? No! Shall we ponder narrative structures and symbolic images? No, let's not! Shall we measure outcomes? No! But – panic! – what have we learned? The magic of a story, that's what. Ask Shaka and his chums. What a cracking yarn. Give it a go. It'll perk up these last weeks. Never fails. With or without Tommy the caretaker.

Don't smile 'til Christmas

Published 7 December 2006

"Don't smile 'til Christmas!" I was once told by a pedagogical sage.

"Not with a new class!" A drear nostrum.

"You're not their friend! Not there to be liked."

Well, yes, but...

I've never quite managed the hatchet face. I give it a go every year. I go for the chill gravitas. The patrician hauteur. Not easy if you look like a bald owl. I did the drill with the new 7th year. First lesson. Line up! Shut up! Hands up! Hats off! Planners out! With my face like a prune. Then I see their cherubic panic – and then I smile. After 5 minutes. The same thing happens when I'm summoned to quell havoc.

"Hello!" they merrily go. I essay the patrician stare.

"Alright then, sir!" I'm not doing "alright". I'm doing thin-lipped terror!

"I see QPR came second again! Quarter Pound of Rubbish!" We are not amused.

"Chill sir! Lighten up!" And I do. I smile.

The sheer wit of pupils – caught in the crossfire of curriculum and boredom and testing – breeds desperate antics like Seth and Rhapsody falling into the sixth pond. Oxbridge scholars! They arrive for my lesson dripping with dank foliage. Or Crumlin and Dillywig hiding in the big flower pot in the staff room and emerging as Bill and Ben.

"Hello Bill! Hello Ben!"

Not big, not clever. I tried hatchet face but had to smile – and put them in the stocks.

This zero tolerance is catching on. The fear patrol seem to rather relish not liking the pupils. They storm the corridors and point their suits at tiny quaking scholars. Mr Stalin roars at Little Walter for being too clever by half. Mr Putin yells at Lily for listening to poetry on headphones. And Miss Strict yells ultimatums at Dillywig because he's there. They're just like my old geography teacher, Mr Morgan. "That's blood on the walls boy! That could be you!"

We were petrified. He cancelled his humanity. He taught us through fear and he taught us nothing. I got seven per cent and thought Caracas was just off Bognor. You can't teach anything this way. Especially English. It trades in the more tender empathies. Fear tends to trump them.

"You must like the children you teach and be able to show them you do," says Philip Beadle. Of course you are in some kind of cahoots with them. Teaching can't work otherwise. This is nothing to do with being "down with the kids." They can see through that.

Anyway my new 7th year seem to be flourishing. Here come the merry crew and here comes the Christmas season.

The voices are back

Published 11 January 2007

I've been at this lark for 30 years but still get nightmares before a new term.

I face blank-faced inspectors who "sledge" me like an Aussie slip field.

"Are you sure you should be doing this?" they go.

I face blank-faced tots who look like something out of "Chucky". Hundreds of them. I am dumbfounded by yards of jargon and gibberish and ultimatums. I must deliver 7-point perfectly paced, differentiating, thrilling, value adding lessons with significant measurable outcomes to maniacs with attention spans of gnats. Or else. Ronald Crumlin walks towards me with his pimp roll.

"Are you sure you should be doing this?" he goes.

I wake up sweating. I pedal to school. I am hailed by dawdling scholars.

"Happy New Year then, sir!"

I pass by my pigeon hole and meet my 10th year tutor set. They charge merrily in. We are pleased to see each other. We all seem to have survived Christmas. What did Santa get us? Rhapsody got a Zadie Smith and Magda got a dictionary. Sabrina got extensions and Lunk got some boots and Dillywig got an iPod which I confiscate. Decibelle got blind drunk and arrested on Shepherds Bush Green – and Crumlin had puppies. Well, his bloodhound did.

"It's a jungle out there. Nasty, brutish and short. But not in our classroom! We're better than that. We will treat each other with kindness. We will not use bad language or take drugs or get pregnant or laugh at Mr Donut. We will work jolly hard and beat those pampered public school boys."

Crumlin and Lunk nod along. "Yo sir!" And off they go ravenous for improvement.

The day is a dream and the pupils quite delightful.

I relax with my chums in the staff room. I go to the pigeon hole. It is chock full of jargon and gibberish and ultimatums and missives from Ms Mumps. I must measure and monitor and update dateline data and "impact on value added" and plan a million perfect lessons and attend C zone teach ins and twilight workshops on performance pre-assessment. By this Thursday. Or else.

It's not the children, it's the admin that gives you the abdabs.

La Batty of Discipline charges towards me in high dudgeon. She's already at volume eleven.

"I need to see Ronald Crumlin and Sidney Lunk about an outrage in the sixth form pond involving Mr Donut and some shaving cream."

I blame me.

"Are you still sure you should be doing this?" go those voices.

I just don't know!

Published 22 March 2007

Alan Bennett – like "Just William" – is sunk on a sofa on *The South Bank Show*. The Lord Bragg – like an anxious pupil – quizzes the great man about Auden. What does he mean? Where would he "place" the Old Scrotum?

Bennett shifts uncomfortably. Melvyn quizzes relentlessly. Bennett sighs and says he's never quite "got" Auden.

"Too difficult! And I'm too lazy!" Melvyn ploughs on. He seems to be mistaking Bennett for the kind of pundit who gives a fig.

"Is he better than Larkin?" "Probably," muses Bennett. "And not merely because one doesn't always understand him." I get the giggles. It's all in those adverbs.

Melvyn has rather had it with this larking. "Why then?" "Oh, Melvyn!" says Bennett in a fit of irritation and giggles. "I DON'T KNOW!"

I wish I could get away with this in my classroom. I feel like Bennett more and more. I'm fed up with this teacher-as-know-all stuff. As peddler of "correct opinion". The slave of the testing and tick box culture which tolerates no ambiguities. Like many teachers I panic and scrawl opinion across a board. It might go thus:

Reasons why Macbeth kills the king. Because he's (a) a loony (b) Scottish (c) both of above (d) henpecked (e) on drugs (f) caught up in a metaphysical existential nightmare. It's atrocious teaching and we all do well. "What's the answer, sir?" says the buffoon Plum. "I DON'T KNOW DENNIS!" The lot you clot. And there's much else I don't know. I don't know why the Ancient Mariner killed that Albatross or why Hamlet didn't get a move on, or whether synthetic phonics make them read, or turkey twizzlers make Plum dumb, or whether fish oil makes Cordelia a genius, or why so many working class pupils still don't go to university, or why QPR can't score a goal, or why Crumlin has the attention span of a gnat and is presently making barking noises under a desk.

I DON'T KNOW!

Even the Oxbridge set get insecure and want some easy answers. We were doing TS Eliot. And he was rather doing for us. We pondered the lines: "Midnight shakes the memory." As a madman shakes a dead geranium.

"Cracking stuff!" "Yes, sir – but what does it mean?" said Rhapsody. I sigh. Fair cop. I've never quite "got" Eliot. A bit difficult. "Why geranium?" She still quizzed. Who know eh? I don't. "Why not chrysanthemum? Rhododendron? Pomegranate?" I give up. "What does it mean, sir?"

"I DON'T KNOW!" Do you? Answers on a postcard please.

And then? And then?

Published 24 January 2008

"He's got skin like a snake and a shiver in his eyes." Blimey!

It's story time. Max Tombs has the 8th year transfixed with one of his dark yarns. He can barely write but my goodness, he can tell a story. This one involves the last tube, a pale stranger, the DeadMan's Handle – and some dread nemesis.

"He's opposite me – a scaly ghost." Aisha puts down her lip balm. "Just me an 'im!" Yasmin is enthralled. "Staring through me – eyes like gobstoppers!" Even Moose perks up.

"I get out at the Grove. Walk down the platform. Look in the driver's cab." Pause. "There is no driver!"

"Oh my days!" says Aisha.

"I pass the canal! I see something pale cross the cold moonlight!"

"Ooer," swoons Marcia.

Story time is the highlight of our week. Real English. They love it. I love it. Just telling tales. No pictures! No PlayStations! No modern nonsense. Just words. Can't beat it. Pure pleasure. Too much pleasure? Should I interrupt? Shall I make a significant pedagogic intervention? We can't have all this unexamined pleasure can we? Are we a bit off syllabus here? You can't measure pleasure.

I once told *The Pardoner's Tale* – it never fails – and Ofsted couldn't measure my competencies. I was a bit short on those measurable outcomes. You have to dissect things. Shall I drone on about demotics, narrative arcs and closures?

"Shall we examine..."

"Let's not, sir!" Let's let Max go on. Let's not dispel the magic. Max should get an A* in telling stories. A crucial skill. The prime minister has just said so: "One of the best anti-poverty, anti-crime policies."

Blake Morrison says so. "Literature is the new Prozac." Eh? We know these things. It's why we teach English.

We deal in stories. Like Pandora's Box, Orpheus and Eurydice, and now Pale Face and the DeadMan's Handle.

"Wh'appen next?"

Max cranks things up. "I walk on – through the dark car park. I pass bins. I hear things in bins. I get in the lift. No lights. Can't see my hand. Then it stops – and I hear breathing..."

"Enough already!" yells Marcia.

"I get home – I shut the door." Max looks around.

"You want a happy ending?"

"Just get on!"

"I double lock it!" Pause. "I triple lock it!" Pause. "Deadlock it! Click on light! Check out the mirror." Pause. "I see a face!" Pause. "It ain't mine! It's him! Him with a shiver in his eyes!"

"Ooh my days!" sighs Aisha.

"And then?"

"You wouldn't want to know!"

It's superteacher!

Published 13 March 2008

A twilight workshop on "outstanding lessons". I hope it's not a bragfest. Bigheads bigging themselves up. Do you have them? Those fellows who come preening into staffrooms and smugly intimate that they're a mix of Jesus and Socrates and Bruce Forsyth. One of Mr Brown's "superteachers".

"I've just had a brilliant lesson with your loony 8th year!"

They're always good with nutters. The ones who throw furniture out of my lessons.

"I got 10 A*s!" No you didn't. Your pupils did.

"I've got Cordelier Swansong into Cambridge!" No. She did.

"Ofsted said I'm an awesome act!"

Oh do shut up! It's poor form.

Good lessons aren't Ofsted snapshots. You know the ones – aims and intentions and starters and pacing and differentiation and interactive gubbins and clinching plenaries.

Learning doesn't happen in 50-minute gobbets. Not in English anyway. You're with a class for 1,500 hours. It shifts and ebbs and flows. In most lessons you're teaching language as weapon of survival. Grammar. Sentences. Clarity. Good lessons are usually happy accidents.

I think I had one the other day – with my brilliant 8th year. They still fizz with insight. You can do anything with them. Like William Blake's *Poison Tree*.

It went thus.

I told them about Blake's life. Sexed things up a bit.

Blake was a local boy. West London. A rebel. In jail for sedition. When they released him, he went walking across Hyde Park. He told a policeman there were "angels in the trees"!

"That's as may be sir."

He was led off to the loony bin.

"Jailhouse to nuthouse in one day!"

"Cool!" said Little Walter.

"Or what?" said the ethereal Kit.

I left them in groups to discuss my whizzo open-ended questions. Their talk was brilliant. Full of hard-earned wisdom and light bulb insight. They didn't rush into glib conclusions. They tolerated ambiguities. They dealt with nuance and complexity. Dizzy and dangerous stuff. You can't measure it. We were still going strong at the pips.

Blimey! Perhaps I'm a "superteacher"! Maybe I should zoom into the staffroom yelling: "I'm so brilliant with my 8th year! I've just got the clot Crumlin into Cambridge! I think I might be an awesome act! Just like Socrates! Pay me lots!"

Next lesson we do noun clusters. Dull. Back to normal. They were rubbish. Me too.

Oh well. William Blake seems to reach those parts that the national curriculum cannot...

A trip to paradise

Published 26 June 2008

My 12th year need a break. They've been doing exams since they could walk. We plan a little jaunt. We need an excuse. An educational alibi. We can't just have pleasure. We must be seen to have targets – measurable if possible.

Got it! We'll combine high culture with a bit of a picnic. We'll go to John Milton's cottage in Chalfont St Giles where he finished *Paradise Lost*. We'll go to the beautiful, rolling Chilterns. But we're not "doing" Milton as a set text! Sshh – we are now. It's his 400th anniversary.

"Our great revolutionary poet!" I declare.

Off we go. We catch the Tube to Marylebone and the train to Seer Green and we're there. We walk though the deep green of Jordan's Woods. I feel compelled to inflict a little learning on them.

"The Mayflower was made from these trees. The Pilgrim Fathers wouldn't have got to America without them."

Almost true.

There's the famous Quaker Meeting House!

"A sanctuary of silence and peace!"

Well, not quite. It's been burned down by hooligans.

We walk through fields and there it is! Milton's cottage. It's tiny and charming. We enter.

"Milton escaped here from the plague of 1665. Blind and persecuted, it was here that he finished *Paradise Lost*. He would compose 40 lines a night and dictate them to his amanuensis."

"Wasn't it a bit dark!" says Nigel dimly.

"A Darkness Visible!" I observe smugly.

We move into the garden. I note the laurels and myrtles and a 17th century sundial. I quote one of my favourite lines: "And all your graces no more use shall have than a sundial in a grave!"

"Great poet, Milton!"

"Er... he didn't actually write that sir!" says the tedious Nigel.

Ah.

"It was John Donne, sir!" he observes. Correctly.

"Whatever!"

That's enough education! Time for our picnic. The class have brought stacks of tuck. We gorge on rare meats, salmon, salads, Stilton, crumbling rolls, strawberries and cream and yards of rather agreeable dry wines. We sit targetless in midsummer's dappled light. Paradise. Then it's evening and back to London. We sit on the Tube.

"Look, sir!" says Almona. A poem on the underground! An extract from *Paradise Lost* – The Expulsion from Eden.

"They looking back, all th' Eastern side beheld. Of Paradise."

What a happy chance! We've just been there too...

Send for Little Kevin!

Published 5 March 2009

This teaching lark requires many roles.

We must be, among other things, vessels of erudition, facilitators of learning, cookers of books and finessers of figures, puppets of

Ofsted, peddlers of plenaries, deliverers of daft curriculums, literacy pogroms, psychotic phonics, and complicit in life-blighting tests. We must be confiscators of hats, mobiles, gum, guns, iPods, and skunk. We must be stand-ups, screws, shrinks, scapegoats, serfs, dress code cops, obesity cops, clap doctors, spin doctors, philosophers, football managers, psychologists, sexologists, hypnotists, post modernists, Creationists, Darwinists, character witnesses, toilet attendants, marriage guidance experts and interactive whiteboard PowerPoint technicians. We must be strict, kind, deaf, caring, brutal – and perfect moral icons.

Multi-tasking? Not half. Still, it's mostly a breeze to us old lags. Except for one role. That of bouncer. Breaker up of fights. I'm rubbish and I'm not alone. Many teachers share this feeling, according to recent "findings" by Select Education. They want help. They want lessons in "restraint techniques" and "positive handling strategies". They're scared of violence and more scared of litigation. Me too. There you are on playground duty and suddenly it all goes Lord of the Flies.

"Your mum! Your God!" Thump! "You smell! You gay!" Thump! The usual dismal mantra. It makes you angry. You move in. "Don't you touch me you poof! Pervert! Paedo!" It's a tricky area.

I got whacked once. Two huge boys were attempting fratricide. I charged in like Clint Eastwood in Spaghetti Westerns. Not easy, when you're five foot, four-eyed and an otherworldly intellectual. "Stop it!" I suggested. Both turned on me.

Thump! Nurse, the screens! Much bruising. No apologies. No union help. Never again. I'm offered a "creative conflict resolution seminar". Eh? I need something more hands on. Aha!

"Little Kevin!" He's 7 feet square. He pumps things. He does martial arts. He kills bricks.

"Never get involved, sir!"

He goes all Zen. He goes into a trance and does a lot of slow motion flailing.

"It's all about attitude," says the muscled sage. Ah. "You haven't got it, sir. Trust me." Ah. "Never ever commit violence!" He does a bit more slow motion stuff.

"But if you do, be first!" He performs a skull-crushing move, with much grunting. He looks up and quotes Sun Tzu. Who he? An ancient Chinese philosopher.

"It's not your job, sir." Quite so.

"Any grief, sir – just send for Little Kevin!" And a few good lawyers.

Chapter 3

In the mode pastoral

'Are you a poof, sir?'

When we're not peddling the canon, the colon, Metaphysical verse, we're meant to be peddling morality. Citizenship. I must be a tutor and pastor and a moral compass for my erring flock. And my 10th year flock are mighty erring. Some of them seem to have transgressed beyond most of the received decencies of Western – or any other civilisation. Lunk for example. Sidney is working towards level seven of Hell. I blame me. So does the *Daily Mail*. I am, they yell, rather too busy promoting original sin, illiteracy, revolution, drugs, homosexuality and the grocer's plural. The 'broken society' was probably broken by me. Someone's got to do it.

I must promote the opposite. I must do the ZERO TOLERANCE.

"Just say no!" I must go.

"Sidney desist! Just say no crime! Be a good citizen!"

Does he listen?

I must be a shepherd to my little children..

"Just say no!"

To sloth, crack, ketamine, amphetamine, scag, skunk and Sunny Delight and happy slapping. No! No! To alco pops, turkey twizzlers, dog burgers, ciggies and Kung Fu Skull Crusher! No! No! To bunking and nicking and dealing and blaspheming and thrilling sex and coca cola and crisps, fish and chips and Carlsberg Special! No! no! And tattoos and graffiti and knee hugging trousers and chilling on street corners and pimp walking and wearing hoodies and ambushing buses and impersonating Spiderman outside Foxtons and putting the frighteners on Mr Donut.

"No No! No!" I go

I look for positives.

"Just say yes!"

To homework, tick boxes, broccoli, carrots, condoms, coursework, pointless drudgery, incurious servility and the business management bollocks that's plastered across the walls.

Do they listen? Not a lot. Pearls before swine.

Still, most are rather good citizens – and rather more moral than their elders.

My own personal drug hell

Published 5 June 2003

"Do you use drugs, Sir?"

I am having problems in the pastoral lesson. We are 'doing' drugs. Would you ask this of the milkman, banker, barber? I didn't join the teaching profession for this 'moral icon' role.

"Have you though, Sir? Smoked weed?"

Of course I haven't. You haven't. We haven't. It doesn't happen. If I even address the subject I might be promoting it. That way madness lies. Or the *Daily Mail*.

"Anything though, Sir?"

Well, there was that fling with the Coca Cola and ash. I was about seven. To escape the pressure of the home counties I dabbled in this hellish brew. We drank it by the bike sheds. It made us feel different – to feeling well.

And there were those times I went down the mean streets of Chalfont St Peter collecting fag ends. We would skin up behind the scout hut. This too induced altered states – a green skin and much puking.

As for the problem with the Tizer – it's still a monkey on my back …

I'm not going to peddle tales of reefer madness and smack hells. Nor suggest a louche empathy with potheads. We need an outside speaker – a mix maybe of Joyce Grenfell and Hunter S. Thompson. Not easy.

I'm not up to it. The pupils know much more than me – about uppers and downers and screamers and things that go whiz – they can get them all over west London. They've always got mashed, bombed, lean and zonked.

It does seem rarer though. Gone are the days when Ned Crumlin would sniff glue off his cuffs to dull the longeurs of my lessons.

We make two lists. In one we note those items which make you dizzy and tedious. In the other we note those which can fell an elephant or make you see crocodiles or become a cabbage.

All things considered, we plump for the dizzy and daft – if you just can't say no, but you must!

I'm not sure I could have done. All those tests and targets would have me back on the Tizer.

I ponder a homily on poverty and alienation and blighted lives – from Gin Lane to crack city.

There still can be no real debate. Until there is, the drug lesson must go thus:

Outside Speaker and I tell class all drugs are bad. Hands up who agrees? Whole class raise hands.

Hands up who has never taken a drug? Whole class raise hands.

Hands up who is never going to take a drug in their life? Whole class raise hands. Hurrah!

"Well done everyone!"

"What – not even weed, Sir?"

Football – the beautiful game

Published 29 January 2004

I'm pushing my bike across the north playground in a grim drizzle after a grim school day. Children zip and zoom about in the floodlights and rain. Loads of them. All kinds. Swots and clots and scholars and bunkers. Differentiation on legs. And they're all performing on level 11.

Without a teacher. It makes the heart sing. It would make Ofsted purr.

"A full range of strategies is being orchestrated," they'd say. Not half.

It's a ballet of tricks and flicks and chips and spins and dummies and shimmies and drag backs and multiple stepovers. Dennis Plum – crippled by the curriculum – is quicksilver through the falling light.

Scarlett times her tackle perfectly, dances past Dervish and drifts the ball perfectly to Charlie on the near post. Poetry in motion.

These pupils are meeting their goals. And some are scoring them. Football. The beautiful game ...

Forget all those fancy workshops – football's the thing. I can teach almost anything through football – especially in English. Prose style? Try whizzo journalists Nick Hornby or Amy Lawrence.

Drama? It's all a theatre of dreams. Jacobean revenge tragedy of blood? Any Man U v Arsenal game. Or Roy Keane's knee-shredding assault on Alfie Haaland. This also covers Machiavellism.

Poetry? Marvell? TS Eliot says he "combines tough reasonableness with a lyric grace".

This befuddles sixth form.

I explain. "Like Bergkamp." Instant illumination.

Existential philosophy? Camus on goalkeeping. Aesthetics? A video of Thierry Henry's recent 'reverse nutmeg' on the dullard Danny Mills. Faster than light.

We could then move on to notions of genius and the utilitarian. Mozart and Salieri. Nor is this lost on girls. Anyway, they've got Totti and Becks ...

Charlie passes the ball to me.

"'Ere Sir! Go on!"

Sad – but I can't resist. I put down the bike and the SATs.

A hush falls on the playground. The rain falls on my glasses.

Shall I attempt the pedestrian outswinger or essay the more difficult and aesthetically pleasing drifter from the outside of the boot? I go for the latter. It drifts and loops and dips past Dervish's flailing limbs. There is a collective gasp.

They can't believe it. Nor can I. I last did this in 1954 against Seer Green Primary School. It was an accident.

"You never really lose it," I inform the gobsmacked Charlie. Respect. I resist the urge to go zooming round with shirt-over-head displaying my 'Scrap SATs!' vest. I pick up the bike. I pick up the SATs. I pedal off into the night.

Using parental control

Published 19 February 2004

I enjoy parents evenings, although the nodding and gravitas can get a bit knackering. The only problems are ...

Not knowing names.

"Nigel is making quantum leaps this term."

"Yeah? How's my Paul doing?"

"Him too."

Or strict grim fathers who bring down wrath of Gods on their trembling daughters if I don't say excellent. I say excellent.

Or Old Man Nerk – Charlie's dad. Charlie is a chip off the old block. He is presently incarcerated in the inclusion unit. I can't tell Nerk the Elder this. He will visit extreme violence on Nerk the Younger.

"Or set the dogs on me!"

I tell the old git that Charlie's doing well. He may well be a genius.

Or you taught them.

"Hello, Sir!

A shining woman beams before me with her beaming daughter.

She has an orchid in her hair and ringlets.

"You still here then?"

I recognise her. It's Zora – aka Beryl the Peril. Late 80s.

"Zora!"

"I'm a Meeja Girl! Remember The Meeja Girls?"

Not half. There were three of them. They used to perfect dance routines to Michael Jackson in my media lessons. We called it Meeja practical.

I was rubbish at the media lesson. Every nutter in the school was in the class. Then we had the inspector in. Panic. She looked like Margaret Rutherford. More panic.

We were deconstructing genres. Utter panic.

"What genre is this?" I quizzed, pointing to men on horses in cowboy hats.

"He's having a laugh!" said Billy.

The inspector examined our folders. She stopped at the Meeja Girls – Zora and Sabrina and Roxanne. Their folders were full of pictures of Michael Jackson. Critical commentary was less than rigorous.

"Whitwham's brill," they told the inspector. "He taught us all we know!"

I was surely doomed. Then they did the moonwalk. The soup kitchen beckoned. They shuffled out at the end of the lesson.

"Don't fancy your chances, Sir!" Nor did I. But the inspector smiled and said she'd really enjoyed herself. Not like today's prune-faced mob. She gave me a whizzo report. The Meeja Girls had saved me. I told Zora her daughter was terrific. This was true.

"Sir, we're all in the foyer!"

They were. All three of them. The Meeja Girls. Parents all.

"Can you still do the moonwalk?"

"Not half."

"Come for a drink, Sir?"

Not half. One of the perks of long service. Parents evenings can be so good.

This is the road to hell

Published 13 May 2004

Three quarters of secondary schools do not have a daily act of collective worship. We are breaking the law. Will we go to hell?

My infants teacher – Mrs Hellfire – would have thought so. She waved two books at us. The Register of Heaven and the Register of Hell. The former was thick. If we did good things we'd get a tick. A billion ticks and we'd go to heaven. The latter was thin. If we did bad things or Had Bad Thoughts, we'd get a cross.

A few crosses and we'd go to hell. I ran around the lawn like a medieval flagellant but could not dispel rude words and visions of naked women – especially that Alma Cogan. I could feel the fires of hell.

My grammar school was no better ...

It was my turn to read the lesson. I was twelve. I clutched the lectern in fear and dread. I gazed out upon the assembled multitudes. I dripped sweat. I became functionally illiterate. I seemed to be swallowing marbles.

I lurched from Shadrach and his fiery furnace to his hanging gardens at Nebuchadnezzar. Unholy gibberish. God was moving in very mysterious ways. I had turned over several pages with my sweating palms. The chaplain glared at me with wrath.

"Here endeth the Lesson!" I muttered. I shuffled off and got cuffed by the boiling theologian. But most of the nodding tots weren't listening. I could have been reciting *Mein Kampf, The Hundred Days of Sodom* or the QPR reserve team – they'd still have said "Amen".

Modern acts of worship are – thank god – less sulphurous. There's every religion in the inner city school – so we go for the secular. This can take many forms. The ranting tyrant, the PowerPoint dude, the sharing anecdotalist – or the vapid new ager who commends hoodlums for not burning the school down during Good Behaviour week. Most fall on deaf ears.

I too must inflict odd pastoral homily on my tutor group. Just say no to sex and drugs and rock 'n' roll and crisps and eat your greens and work jolly hard if you don't want to be a tramp or derelict, are my general themes.

Then I walk amongst my godless flock and wake them up. I'm rubbish. Maybe I should perk things up like Mrs Hellfire and talk in tongues like a snake waving southern preacher.

"Y'all gonna do that coursework now or you gonna burn in hell and snakes gonna eat your eyes out!"

Collective acts of worship are no easy gigs. "Axe them!" says chief inspector Bell. I agree.

Until then I must plod on with my PSHE lessons. I am tempted to unleash some reflections from Kierkegaard or Molesworth or the Venerable Bede. If no one's going to listen – it may as well be to something good.

Suspended animation

Published 14 October 2004

I'm sipping a cappuccino in my favourite Italian café. It's the middle of a Monday morning and the highlight of my day. Until I see Dave Hooligan sipping a cappuccino.

He's sitting over there under a picture of Juventus with froth upon his nose. I hide behind my *Guardian*. He hides behind his hood. He sees me seeing him. Shouldn't we both be in school? Aren't we both truants? I must acknowledge him. I give him a whey-faced smile.

"Shouldn't you be in school David?"

"No Sir – as it happens. Suspended, Sir!"

"What for this time?"

"Bunking, Sir." He adds four sugar lumps.

"You get sent home if you're caught! And I can't stay home. My mum would kill me if she found out!" He removes hood.

"What's your excuse then, Sir?"

"I'm part time. I don't work Mondays."

I'm downshifting. Redressing the life–work balance. Dave too it seems – although he's always erred on the first part of the equation.

"Alright for some, Sir!"

"Why do you keep bunking?"

"Too much grief, Sir – I can't hack it anymore!' He delivers a rather trenchant diatribe on current pedagogical fashions. It is in the tradition of Illich, Rousseau and the Bash Street Gang. He's bored senseless by the national curriculum, he's not meeting his targets and his school career is in freefall.

Snap. We drift into a rather unprofessional complicity.

"You go mental, Sir!" And all that testing is the final straw. He couldn't face that last one. Hid in the toilets, got picked up on the CCTV and then he bunked it. He gets up and pulls up his hood. The froth is still upon his nose.

"Can't hang about. Be lucky then, Sir!" He's gone. Off to do dodgy deals under Shepherd's Bush – or to just sit on a wall under the Westway with earthquakes in his ears and wait until his mother gets home. Anything's better than another chance to fail …

I'm sipping another cappucino next Monday. So is Dave Hooligan. Again. Will no one rid me of this turbulent youth?

"What is it this time?"

"Locked out, Sir!"

"By whom?"

"The school, Sir – cos I was late!"

"Why were you late?"

"You know. The usual. All the fighting and the dogs." More sugar lumps. "The bouncers lock the gates after nine, Sir."

Those gates are about 30 feet high with daggers at the top.

"Tried to climb in. Nearly got over! Nearly lost my bollocks, Sir!" Ah – what a lust for learning!

"So I legged it Sir!"

"But you're bunking again!" Should I grass him?

"Had to – innit! If they'd caught me they'd have sent me home!"

Well – should I?

The great outdoors

Published 7 April 2005

Cell block 101 is more than usually dismal. The world outside is more than usually radiant. Daffodils dance, blossoms burst, bunnies jump and bunkers frolic in the sixth form gardens. We are feeling more than usually incarcerated.

My class has zero tolerance of auxiliary verbs and temporal connectives. Me too. Spring is raging. So are my pupils. We should all be outside. We should all perhaps be on a school trip. They're a Good Thing. Ruth Kelly says so.

"Trips," she drones, "encourage outdoor learning, confidence and increase skills."

I must jot this down. I've been on many school journeys over the years.

Our treks beyond the Iron Curtain were groundbreaking. They were also blue murder. Our journey through Checkpoint Charlie could have been our last. The guards didn't always share our robust cockney wit. It wasn't easy explaining that V signs were peace signs.

And pre-Glasnost Moscow was even worse. The KGB had the same humour bypass as the Stasi. The free west was scarcely better. Our sojourn in Paris may have been culturally enriching, but the travel agent could have told us that our hostel was probably a bordello.

Our English jaunts have had similar tensions. Of course it's a Good Thing for the posses of Ladbroke Grove to be let loose over the rolling hills of Dorset. I'm all for it. But the open spaces can make them nervous. They can retreat into alcohol and … sshh … class C drugs.

Boys drink vodka and cider and sing Motorhead songs and fall into comas or the sea or drift off in pedalos towards distant horizons or – on one occasion – steal an eel from Lyme Regis Aquarium.

Girls drink alcopops and babycham and essay romances with muscled buffoons or fairground hoodlums. Decibelle once dragged Lunk into the Tunnel of Love at Margate's Dreamland.

They didn't surface for hours. Lunk may well have been learning new skills. He may well have learned new confidence. Both may well have been illegal. Luckily conception did not occur.

I'm always the fall guy. The killjoy. The buffoon apologising to coach drivers, coppers, bouncers, guides, guards, curators, fairground attendants, gendarmes, the secret police and the KGB. I'm always in loco parentis. It wears me out. I end up merely loco.

So, no. I will forego the next school journey. We'll have a picnic instead – in the sixth form gardens. We leave cell block 101 and our auxiliary verbs for a little outdoor learning under those dancing blossoms.

Boys in the hood

Published 9 June 2005

A special assembly has been called. A deputy head rakes tots with a fierce gaze. A pupil is also on the stage – exhibit A. The head fulminates sulphorously.

"You will wear caps! You will wear hats! You will wear black shoes! Not brothel creepers! You will wear your hair short! If you don't, matron will cut it off! You will look like me!"

We don't want to look like Gilbert Harding …

"You will not look like that!"

He points at exhibit A. He is Martin Priestly. He looks like Elvis Presley. He's a folk devil. Dangerous. Cool. He has no hat and long hair and brothel creepers. He is sent to matron – a formidable woman – who will cut things off. We are dismissed …

It is 1962. We're in a posh grammar school. I am a pupil. I swore I'd never be part of such a system.

Forty odd years on … A special assembly has been called. A deputy head rakes tots with a fierce gaze. A pupil is also on the stage – exhibit B. The head fulminates sulphorously.

"You will not wear baseball caps! You will not wear hoods! You will wear black shoes! Not trainers! You will not wear your hair short! If you do wear hoods, Miss Batty will cut them off! You will look like me!"

They don't want to look like Oliver Letwin.

"You will not look like that!"

He points at exhibit B. He is Ronald Crumlin. He looks like Eminem. He's a folk devil. Dangerous. Cool. He has a hood and a number one and trainers. He is sent to Miss Batty – a formidable woman – who will cut things off. They are dismissed ...

We are in a modern inner-city comp. I am a teacher. I am part of this system. I'm part of another moral panic. I care not a fig what they put on their bonces. Trilbies or tea cosies or pork pies or 10-gallon hats or feathers or periwigs or homburgs – or the dread hoods.

But I must be seen to care. I ditch starters for dress code rants – especially with the 10th year. Here come my little hooded chums ... Mooch and Lunk and Ace and Dervish all sport the Snoop Dogg look. They look like the four Horsemen of the Apocalypse. Decibelle sports a wimple. She looks like my granny.

"Hoods off! Hoods off!" I bark.

"Liberties!" They are removed.

"And you Crumlin!"

"Can't, Sir – against my religion." Ho! Ho!

There's only one solution to the hood problem. Make them compulsory. I feel a plenary coming on. I fulminate sulphorously.

"Tomorrow you will all wear hoods!"

"Liberties, Sir!"

"Or you'll be on the chain gang in orange pyjamas!"

Anywhere but school

Published 6 October 2005

I take the register. Friday pm. There's a lot of absences.

"Where's Lunk?"

"He got court!"

"Furnace?"

"Gotta see his dad!"

"And Crumlin?" "Birdflu, Sir!" Ho bloody ho.

And Lily?

Where are they? Bunking. Fleeing the tedium. Fleeing the dread curriculum. It's all the go. Worse than ever. They're slinking off through school gates and climbing over walls.

They're shivering on swings in the drizzling rain. Or sharing a Coke and chips in McDonalds. Or sipping on Tennents in Meanwhile Gardens or shoplifting in Whiteleys or huddled in the shadows under Westway. All dodging the coppers and the taggers and patrols.

"I'm on a fieldtrip ... a visit ... it's sportsday." In October? I fear for them – prey to dodgy deals and so many dread distractions. Furnace is down the 'Bello having a tattoo. Roxanne is nicking things in Boots. And Crumlin's playing footie against a carpark wall. And this is better than my scintillating lessons? I get depressed.

Where is Lily? Who sits pale and wan at the back reading *The Heart is a Lonely Hunter*? Not here. Her mother dropped her at the station this morning – but she took another tube to spend the day with Cordelia Swansong. They sit smoking spliffs on a sofa.

They're listening to Babyshambles or it might be Nick Drake. They must come back, they must meet their dreary targets. Clever lost girls bunking the brute inner-city world. Can I blame them? When so much must be so dull?

I truanted – from the Royal Grammar School, High Wycombe. I bunked Chunk Jones' French lesson.

"I'd rather teach a vegetable than you!" he barked. So I bunked off with Brian Rumble. We slunk off to The Record Shack to listen to the Shangri Las and gaze upon the bunking high school girls. We thought we were cool outlaws. Mr Plod didn't. He dragged us back to school.

Mr Jones didn't. He called us "wide boys" and hit us with a stick. Never again. We were soon back. But I'm not sure about Furnace and Roxanne and Crumlin – and the very gifted Lily. Will they get back on track?

The lesson is a whiz because the nutters have all scarpered.

I must phone the home of every bunker. I start with the Crumlin. He answers.

"Heh man wha' 'appen?"

I inform him that his English teacher is happening. He pretends to be his dad. He has no dad.

"He got birdflu, man." Ho bloody ho. I ring up Lily's mum. No reply. They will all be suspended. It's what you get for bunking.

Young hearts run free

Published 4 May 2006

Spring breaks out. So does Malcolm "Sex God" Perkins. Where is he?

Hormones rage. So do I. Where's Decibelle? With Perkins I shouldn't wonder. Canoodling in the sixth form gardens again.

They're missing my starter on Romeo and Juliet. Rather essential.

They shuffle in. "Sorry we're late, Sir!" "Detention! Both of you!" No time for sentiment.

Last week Dragana didn't do the homework. "I got love issues!" she sighed. As if I care! "Detention!" No time for these mawkish distractions.

"You're just jealous, Sir!" says Yasmin. "And, anyway, Romeo and Juliet were 14!"

"And they never had homework!" chimes Sabrina.

"It was different in those days."

"It wasn't though!" She's right. It's very like Shepherd's Bush. We have lively discussions on sex and drugs and rock'n'roll. They're easy and open about these matters. Emotionally intelligent. Boys and girls together.

But don't they distract each other? Girls do better without boys. But boys do better with girls. Should we separate them?

I'm not sure. Others are – like those on Channel 4 *That'll Teach 'Em*. They want to go back to the 50s and single sex schools.

Well, I went to one. Academically we were top dogs. Emotionally we were top clots. The sex lesson was conducted by a severe botanist – Mr Mail.

"But I am not a bee!" cried the desperate Brian Rumble.

Girls got into the school just the once. Pressganged from Wycombe High for dance classes. This occurred in the gym with Mr Jones of PE – a grim Methodist from the Welsh valleys. He had a blackboard and Dansette.

At one end was a litter of forlorn boys. At the other a gaggle of forlorner girls. We were ordered to couple.

We scuttled around until natural selection occurred. The lookers soon found each other. The plain shambled together. The rest of us met in a disowning glare – girls wept by wall bars and we polished shoes on grey flannels.

"Dance! Dance! And I want to see light between your bodies."

We tottered around each other like a bomb disposal unit. Anything erogenous and we might go off. Brian Rumble did. Mr Jones came down on him with Pentecostal wrath.

You don't easily recover from this single sex stuff. You might spot us at parties. Pale and shuffling and emotionally illiterate.

Co-education must be better. Malcolm and Decibelle think so. They're early for my detention. It's just another lovers' tryst.

Getting in the thick of it

Published 21 September 2006

"Peter is a cretin."

I write on a report. Nothing else.

I sign it. I gaze at it. A tiny sentence on a big page. Perfecto! It has a Swiftian precision. Unambiguous. Unvarnished. Those hard Ts are most effective.

"Peter is a cretin."

This is untrue. He is not a cretin. He is bright and much troubled. So am I. By him. He has a PhD in winding me up. For years. He is a creator of chaos and a promoter of migraine. He always wins. This time I will get him. I will have a moral holiday. It makes me feel better. I ponder the context and have a laugh. It is so wrong. So offends our caring culture. I imagine the second takes. I imagine parents' evening. I wonder how it will play with his mother. Or with the *Daily Mail.*

"Trendy lefty hippy teacher in showpiece comprehensive calls gifted child a cretin."

I'm usually so positive. I big up hoodlums. They need all the breaks they can get. Not this time.

"Peter is a cretin!"

All jobs must have this saloon bar stuff. A safety valve. Not for public consumption I thought. I was wrong. Blogger Frank Chalk now has a book. I enjoy much of it. Then I stop laughing.

"The kids are thick, the parents are scum, there are drugs everywhere, and half the girls are giving birth."

This is untrue. Children with "learning difficulties" are also called "thick".

I can get this stuff elsewhere. From the *Mail* or Melanie Phillips or Sir Digby Jones or the odious Jimmy Carr – or from the chattering salons of Notting Hill. It's all the rage. They all insult my pupils whom they will never meet. They are "feral, illiterate, innumerate, unemployable, yobs, thugs." Sir Digby says they're hopeless for business. This makes me rather proud of them. They are not the cogs of capitalism.

You make them weak and then you hurt them. You label them "thick" and then you wonder why they go bonkers? They are many things – "thick" isn't one of them. You'd have to be a bit thick not to realise this. They occupy other literacies – probably the wrong ones. Sir Digby should pop into my 10th year sometime and hear Sabrina, Albert and Peter talking about Shoot the Messenger or Timothy Winters, or whether Wenger must have a plan B. It's incisive and vital – and, alas, unacknowledged.

I wouldn't fancy Sir Digby's chances. Or Blogger Frank's.

And most aren't stoned or with child.

It's cheap and easy. Like me. I will revise things.

"Peter is NOT a cretin."

In the mode pastoral?

Published 12 October 2006

I'm walking through Notting Hill after school. Past the posh emporiums and modish fashion palaces. There's a kerfuffle on the street. Youths frolic in front of Faust's Estate Agents. One smudges his grim visage against the glass. Another hooded Herbert scales the windows like Spiderman. A third, trousers round his knees, yells "One billion! I'll have it!" Is this street theatre? A French mime troupe? Hip anti-capitalists?

Nope. It's Sidney Lunk and the Dillywig twins. Messing about. It's just a public nuisance. I blame me. I am their tutor.

The estate agents are not amused. Tufty haired fellows with yellow ties, they peddle properties we can't afford. They glower from screens and curse and shoo away the hooded apparitions. To no avail. The grotesque pantomime continues. Dillywigs cavort and Lunk makes like Quasimodo. That citizenship module doesn't seem to have caught on.

What a resonant little tableau! Little Britain indeed! Spivs v hooligans.

Shall I wend my way regardless? No. I must be professional. I must intervene. I hail them. I suggest they desist. And reluctantly they do.

"They're tossers tho' innit sir!"

I apologise to Tufties who regard me with contempt.

I see them next day in tutor set. In PSHE. I've never liked PSHE. We used to do Big Issues. I used to do Homilies. They went thus. Bunking. Burgers. Drugs. Sloth. Sex – BAD! Swotting. Wheat germ. Greens. Exercise. Condoms – GOOD! They'd smile and nod and then bunk off and eat Fat Boy Burgers or sneak into the back seats of the Coronet ...

Now it's a greyer area. Now I must do life skills. We must learn to be cogs of capitalism. We must learn how to present ourselves in the business world. We must join the cutting, thrusting, multi-tasking, soft-skilled electronic global village. We must to be like the groovy fellows of Faust's. I don't feel good about this. I was raised on Marx and Marcuse and Paul Goodman. On work as "alienation" and "teaching as a subversive activity". On broader views of education. Now I must turn the raging glory that is Sidney Lunk into a clot with a yellow tie.

I give them all a bollocking. This bad behaviour might end up on their CVs. "It's not big or clever or funny!"

"All property is theft, eh sir!"

"You were laughing tho' sir!"

Well. Yes. A bit. The spiderman was rather droll. And I know whose side I'm on come the revolution.

Nuff gays innit sir?

Published 17 May 2007

The 10th year have been charging through *A View from the Bridge*. We're cruising along nicely at Ofsted level 1. They love it. It hits all the buttons. Machismo, Mafia, immigrants, feisty girls, and heavy manners. Little Italy – it's just like Shepherd's Bush.

"Who wants to read?" Almost everybody. Especially those who can't. Like Sidney Lunk and Dragana. I must be kind. Others aren't.

"Not Sidney! Jesus! Life's too short, sir!" I must give them a go. They're quite hopeless. It's like swallowing marbles.

"Jesus sir! He's got them special needs innit!"

So we go back to yesterday's cast. That's Magda from Prague as feisty girl. Dillywig from the Grove as cool paramour Rodolpho. "As if!" mutters Sabrina. And me as Eddie Carbone – in rather well-honed Tony Soprano mode. And Decibelle and Sabrina as a gossiping Greek chorus.

"I wouldn't put up with it! Do what you want girl! Lipstick? Short skirts? Whatever! Don't make you a slapper!" Rhapsody sighs. She's a post-feminist.

Then we get to the dread scene. It demands so much emotional literacy. "Eddie kisses Rodolpho." Shock! Horror! Most can deal with it. Girls can. Some boys can't. Dillywig can't. He refuses to read on. There are bonehead ruminations.

"Footballers kiss when they score though!" "Not at QPR they don't!" "That's 'cos they don't score!" "Poofs!" mutters Furnace, "we shouldn't be doing this!"

Homophobia is rife these days. I feel compelled to have a rant. Furnace has had enough of me. I irk him. "Nuff gays innit sir!"

I have had enough of him. He irks me. I should go deaf. I don't. I attempt to explore "gay". I talk of the damage words can cause. I go grey with rage. They go solemn. Some tell Furnace to "shut it".

"I'll see you afterwards Anthony!" "Whey hey!" he says.

We try to get back to the scene.

"Are you a poof, sir?" Furnace is a victim of his culture. I should challenge this laddish behaviour, but what's the point? I can't take on fundamentalist religions and tabloid culture and gangsta rap and the *Daily Mail*. I have another rant.

"But are you sir? A poof?" Pause. "I'll tell you what I am, Anthony. Tired. Tired of all this rubbish! I've heard it for the last 30 years!"

"But are you though?" I am now ashen with rage. I must not lose it. I must be professional... I lose it.

"Shut up you tedious heterosexual!"

"You can't say that! I could have you done, sir!"

Bring out your Bunters!

Published 27 September 2007

"Bring out your fatties! Bring out your Bunters!" Oh no! It's the government Fat Wagon in the playground again. The obesity police are here. The Ed Balls boys. It's not just SATs these days. It's fats too. Some of my 8th years quake in their boots.

Quick! Quick! Hide! I must hide Thomas Plum and Tessie O'Shea in a cupboard or they'll be carted off to a fat camp. We lost Waller last week. Too wide. The poor round boy was torn from his wailing mother's arms. Pitiful stuff.

Bang! Crash! The door's kicked in! They storm in. Three of them. The Fat Police – with dogs and prods and speak-your-weight machines.

"Who ate all the pies? Come on, let's 'ave yer! Out with those lunchboxes!"

Out they go on every desk. Full of junk food. Now banned by Balls. Illicit stuff. Like Antic Pies, Bloody Offal, Hash Loonies, Acne Pizzas, Coca Comas, Red Mists, Dr Manias and Dog Burgers smuggled by mothers through railings. All confiscated.

Imogen and Hector escape – with their fennel and fish oil and pulses and pomegranate. They sit there slender and smug and organic.

Tiny eyes strafe our classroom. They stop at the cupboard. A bit of bum is sticking out! The bum of Plum. It's too large. It falls out. He falls out. He is dragged onto a hammock and poked and weighed.

"Fifteen and three pounds! Fifteen and three pounds!" shrieks the machine.

He blubbers down his chins.

"Gotcha! It's a bunter!"

He is stripped half bare and branded a "bunter" on his bellies. He's put in a sack and a wheelbarrow and a stair lift and tipped into the Fat Wagon. I see his moon face weeping against the windows as it pulls away.

"Any more? You! You look a bit of a porker!"

Toby Plod is put on the machine. He is borderline and is saved by his speed habit.

All this Jamie Oliver stuff will never take. You create an underclass and peddle it junk for years and then you ban it and tell them to eat seaweed and lentils. Fat chance! The School Food Trust says the healthy lunchbox might contain "chicken tortilla wrap with sweet pepper and carrot and tomato slices and mixed vegetable rice salad".

Well, of course. But it will take ages.

"We'll be back next week!" bark the obesity police.

Tessie comes out of the cupboard. Like Anne Frank. A very wide Anne Frank. She is shaking. She's next up for the chop. Well, liposuction – unless she loses half her bodyweight.

Fat chance!

Chapter 4

Some pupils

'I never let my schooling interfere with my education'

Tiny pupils line up in silence on their first day of Big School. They stand in the clean, dappled light of a big chestnut tree all scrubbed and shining and a bit scared. It always does me in. You'll have them for 5 years. 1500 hours. You look at their faces down the line. Who'll be alright? Who won't? Who'll go daft? Look at them. Children from suburb, ghetto, high-rise, low rise, hostel, hotel, bed, embassy or King Hell Mansions. What a rich mix of souls. Off they go down the torrent of their fates.

Most will be fine. Good. Decent. Sorted. Successful. They can be a bit invisible in the inner-city classroom. And these pages. I don't celebrate them enough. Instead we find the larkers and bunkers and holy fools and exiles and the damaged. My more illustrious scholars. I'm amazed how much they're disliked. How often they're shrunk to a *Daily Mail* cartoon. They're 'thugs', 'yobs', 'feral'. Folk devils. Urban myths. Of course some are bloody maniacs. You wouldn't want Sidney Lunk on a wet Thursday afternoon. Of course they're half daft – so would you be living in King Hell Mansions. A measurable outcome in a dull curriculum. A 'D–'. A 'failure'. Well, they're not failures. They inhabit different literacies. Some literacies are rewarded and some aren't.

Throughout it all loiters Ronald Crumlin. A modern day Nigel Molesworth. Wit. Philosopher king. Clot. Crumlin was a real pupil but he seems to have become a bit generic. Crumlins flourish throughout the nation. I bet he's standing in that line of tinies – ready to see off most schemes of improvement. He's bit of a hero. Like Huckleberry Finn.

"They're going to adopt me and sivilse me and I can't stand it."

Seeking asylum from boredom

Published 16 October 2003

It's Jiri's first day in my school. Probably any school. For Jiri is a traveller who has fled the Czech Republic. He has exchanged the bleak terrors of Prague for the drear horrors of a hostel in Queensway. A rotund boy of 14, he sits down and chews gum and smiles at me like Oliver Hardy.

I smile back. We wave at each other.

I've been to Prague.

"A magical city!" I tell him. "The Golem! Kafka! Patrick Berger!"

He looks at me as if I am a cretin. I am a cretin. They are building a concentration camp just outside the city. For gypsies.

A few weeks later and Jiri sits just sullen and chewing. He falls off the horse in gym. He lugs an accordion into the foyer and is sent home. He's late for every lesson because he gets lost. Teachers shout at him. He becomes a nomad of the corridors.

Headteachers shout at him. This makes him late. I shout at him. I put him on 'late report'. This must be signed at the end of every lesson. This makes him late for every lesson. Even more shouting.

So he sits on the stone lions in the south playground playing an accordion. This is also wrong. He gets a letter home. His mum doesn't understand it. It gets translated. She whacks him on the head.

"Fuck this for a game of pilchards!" he probably muses in Romany.

Then he bunks off. He gets suspended for this. He gets kicked out for being absent. I fail to explain. He bunks off some more. Then he goes AWOL and busks down the Portobello Road. Education welfare officers and coppers and snitches and the *Daily Mail* are on his case.

It's just like the secret police.

He's carted back. He's now quite mute. During *Stig of the Dump* he gets dangerously bored. He puts gum into Decibelle's hair. He is convulsed with mirth. She is convulsed with rage.

She attempts to get rid of the stuff but only spreads it more widely over her skull. She zooms off to the school nurse who cuts lumps off her locks. Poor Decibelle returns looking like Robert Plant on a bad hair day. No one dares to laugh.

"Where's my highlights gone, then?"

Jiri gets a long suspension.

He makes one more appearance – for an English test.

"Aj count du the exam," he scribbles and totters off into oblivion.

That was all two years ago. We had so few support teachers. Now there's fewer. And many more Jiris seeking some kind of asylum.

Last week I met a band of wandering minstrels in Soho. They were playing the sad airs and crazed jigs of Eastern Europe. They were making a gorgeous racket. A rotund boy was chewing gum and playing some killer accordion. He smiled at me like Oliver Hardy.

"Alright then, Sir?"

Seth and the KGB

Published 21 October 2004

"Could you fill it in please, Sir?"

Seth Whitehawk hands me a yellow report. You get these for serious misdemeanours.

"I'm on community service!"

He must sweep up litter and leaves and be nice to tinies for a whole week. Seth is a hugely bright, floridly bonkers middle class boy. His mother – liberal, battered and decent – worries herself daft about him.

He shuffles and nods in front of me. Seth lives on the edge of the dress code – and mostly everything else. His crumpled clothes fall over his gawky limbs. His lank poetic locks cover his delicate visage.

He looks as if he's escaped from Gormenghast. He is generally hidden in a stock cupboard on open days. I write 'excellent' on his report.

He's always excellent. He mesmerises us with his anecdotes and acting. He was a brilliant Oberon in the school play.

I like Seth. He makes me laugh. But he gets us into trouble ...

Enter Big Wigs in our classroom. We are having our millionth inspection. Big Cheese locates Seth and his exercise book, a crumpled ruin covered with tiny plasters and gothic scribbles of blood and the word AAARGH!

Seth finds this droll. I find this droll – in a Molesworth sort of way. Big Wigs do not find this droll. They find it tiresome. It could well reflect woefully low pedagogical expectations.

"Immature and unacceptable!"

I concur. They pass his book around. It is written in Martian, in an erring, inchoate filigree scrawl. It looks like pressed spiders.

I do a lot of concurring. Seth looks at me sternly.

"But I'm dyslexic!" he yells.

"True!" I bleep. "Just like Eddie Izzard."

Exit Big Wigs going "Harrumph!"

"What's this yellow card for?"

"I was on the roof, Sir!"

"Big Ben? Buckingham Palace? 'Kids SA no 2 SATs'?"

"School sir. Climbed up for assembly! Not allowed in!"

"You're not usually that keen!"

"Wanted to see the King of Russia."

Mr Gorbachev was visiting the school. Seth's mum told him to see the great man. The security patrol caught him – or was it the KGB? – and carted him away.

A rather splendid act!

"Don't do it again!" I drone.

He's off to meet his gaunt chums in their patch. They laugh or zip around brilliantly on skateboards or listen to dystopian lyrics at plane crash volume. Just like Seth. Middle class children in the inner city comp. They duck and weave and go half barmy between the brutalities of the inner city and the disenchantments of the curriculum.

Me too.

Getting Plum a 'C'

Published 14 April 2005

There has been an enormous amount of activity around Dennis Plum of late. He has become the epicentre of a pedagogical cyclone. The fate of the school may rest on Plum.

He is of huge statistical significance. The portly feckless fellow is a 'D' grade in most of his subjects. He is on the dull cusp of failure. He cares not a fig.

Plum is the national average on legs. One fears for the nation. In English he's still not on top of conditional tenses or transitional paragraphs. He still uses the grocers' plural.

His oral work is Beckhamesque. His art is worse than primitive. He flirts with a 'C' in food technology – he's a bit of a whizz with marzipan cakes but he's rubbish on the theory. And in resistant materials he is resistant material.

He's got his exams in June. We must shift the Plum to 'C' grades. For all our sakes. If Plums fail so do we. If Plums succeed so do we. We go up the league table. We avoid relegation. It's like managing Norwich.

Significant strategies are unleashed upon him. He must attend twilight working parties. With his mum. It's not her idea of fun. There's not a lot of dancing. And she has, apparently, spawned a moron.

He must attend holiday workshops. Another oxymoronic hell. He could be chillin' under the Westway. He must attend Easter revision classes. He must revise everything that he knows. "Shouldn't take long, Sir!" Ho ho.

He must be bombarded with crib sheets and panic answers and bitesize bullet points and boatloads of worksheets. The very opposite of education.

How many facts can the little vessel take? Will the poor mite go bonkers? No chance. He is fecklessly immune to every grim intervention. Plum may be a 'D' but he's probably an A* in sanity. These panic strategies don't work on him. They didn't work on me either

I was a Plum at maths. A rather unambiguous 'D' grade. I had to get a 'C' to get to university. And to keep my school top of the league tables. I too had to attend revision classes. Booster lessons for cretins with Mr 'Chunk' Jones – a Welsh Pentecostalist.

He accused me of deliberate ignorance. He was wrong. I was merely thick. He shouted at me. To no avail. I was bombarded with boatloads of worksheets. I still couldn't do cosines or quadratics – and much else.

He threw a board duster at my head. I had to go to hospital. I was pronounced concussed – and probably innumerate

I somehow fluked a 'C' grade. I went to university. I became a teacher – who must get Plum a 'C' grade. Then he too could perhaps become a teacher. And teach Plums. Lucky him.

E's a jolly good fellow

Published 8 September 2005

It's GCSE results day. I feel compelled to attend. So does Dennis Plum – with even less relish. We meet at the school gates.

"Good morning!" I say.

"I don't think so," he says.

We walk through the sixth form gardens. Girls frolic in the rhododendrons. They hug and wave A grades. Boys punch the air like Flintoff getting Gilchrist. Others look most woebegone and sob and slump under the school sign.

"Seeking genius in people" reads the school motto. I'm just seeking C grades in Dennis Plum. Plum who has no room or books or father but only Mrs Plum the cleaner who can barely cope. He plods towards the foyer like a condemned man.

For 5 years I've tried to render her son, who is in no way stupid, functionally literate. I've tried any old method ... Look and yell. Incarceration. Bribery. Death threats. I've tried a few fashionable ones – synthetic, kinetic, and latterly psychotic, phonics. Nothing ever took. He remains an inviolate E.

But we must get 40% A–Cs. If we don't Mr Ofsted will bin us.

So we stream – and hothouse borderline Cs. And the rest? The Plums? We bin them in the bottom stream with chaos and cover teachers and no support. Like many schools ...

Plum picks up the dread envelope.

"Go on open it!" "Yeah go on!"

He saunters past Crumlin and Furnace – clever nutters, they clutch a raft of Es. Past Sabrina.

"What does X mean?" she wonders.

He saunters past me. I flinch. I resent being complicit in this carnival of inequality. This trauma of labels. It seems I don't teach any more. I merely test. I divide and fail so many decent children. It's like my own 11+ results so long ago when I punched the air and left my blubbing chums forever.

"Good luck!" I tell Dennis.

"Oh come on, Sir!" he says.

He plods off alone. He treks to Kensal Rise canal. He regards the poison waters. He regards the poison missive. Go on Dennis! Open it! Wouldn't it be nice if it said Cs and Plum got to Blair's Promised Land? Instead of another kick in the brains.

He looks one last time at the envelope. He does not open it. He knows. He's known from reception class. I know too. And so do you. He tears it up. And casts the bits across the toxic waters. And watches those rubbish grades drift away. He goes home.

"How d'yer get on love?" says the careworn Mother Plum.

The invisible ones – Geena and Lily

Published 17 November 2005

I'm lugging the trolley round Sainsbury's – maybe I should nick it for the weekend marking – and move up to the check-out girl. She looks up.

"Yo! Sir!" It's Geena! She was in my sixth form class 3 years ago.

Bright and shy and scared silent by the clever clogs. There were no books at home. No time or silence. And no money. She had to work and cook and care for her sick mother and three brothers. She was on D grades. No good for the league tables.

She got depressed. Then she got vodka drunk in the sixth form gardens. Then she got kicked out. And I thought we were a comprehensive. What's so wrong with D grades? You can become a teacher with D grades. But now she's smiling.

"Got A grades Sir! At Richmond College Sir!"

"Well done! Fantastic!" She just needed more time.

"Are you at university?"

"Can't afford it, Sir!"

The man behind me in the queue gets angry. So do I.

She waves goodbye. I'd wave back but I'm burdened by bags.

She just disappeared. A lot do

Like Lily in my 10th year. She sits mute as a Buddha. She's a bit invisible. The quiescent can get invisible in my school – you forget their names on parents evenings.

Lily isn't a florid histrionic or a hoodie or a bunker or a yeller or bonkers. She doesn't talk in italics or in East LA or the Bronx. She's not with Ms Limpet the shrink or the gifted and talented or the otherwise conspicuous.

I see her alone in the west playground eating rocket sandwiches and rapt to her headphones. Otherwise she's off my radar.

Until last Friday. I'm lugging a ton of assessment sheets home – after another compelling twilight workshop. I pass the assembly hall. I hear someone pounding a piano from behind the curtains.

Real Boogie Woogie. Who is this? Meade Lux Lewis? Jerry Lee Lewis? Nope. It's Lily, that's who. Bashing out the barrelhouse piano. I recognise the tune – Honky Tonk Train Blues. I love this stuff.

"Fantastic Lily! Fantastic!"

"Thank you Sir!" I make a request – Whole Lotta Shakin' Goin' On. Her fingers dance across those ivories. Brilliant! But I must leave. She waves goodbye. I'd wave back but I'm burdened by assessment.

Boogy Woogie Lil! And A grade Geena! Who would have known? Not me. Too busy with the maniacs. Too busy with the league tables. And much too busy assessing them to find out who they are.

A reason to be cheerful

Published 24 January 2006

I pedal to school of a drear and cheerless morning. I buy *The Guardian*. I glance at the tabloids. They are at full throttle about education.

I read of "paedos" and perverts and "porno sirs" and rubbish teachers and millions of illiterates and feral hoodies happy slapping and prime ministers hosing down graffiti.

Crumbs! No one seems to like schools.

Mere hysteria. Shrill pundits are keen to tell me why they cannot sacrifice their middle class children to their liberal principles and to an inner-city school like mine.

Well, they should meet Ollie in my sixth form. Ollie is that middle class child. And Ollie is a reason to be cheerful. He is beaming at me and waving a letter.

Ollie lives with his single mother – a midwife from St Mary's. A wise woman, she's chosen to sacrifice little Ol on the altar of her liberal principles.

Little Ol has always been as bright as a pin and a bit of an intellectual.

I've taught him for 7 years. Well, we've been in the same classroom. I've tried to be a sort of benign witness. He has sat there with a Zen calm and rather relished the florid extremities of our class. And the class rather relished him. He could read most of *Romeo and Juliet* for us and Decibelle and Sabrina just swooned.

Crumlin and Furnace soon stopped calling him a poof.

"Respect!" they said with furrowed brows. "He's deep!"

He ducked and weaved and wobbled and sometimes even bunked.

He might have dabbled in the gentler drugs. Like boys do. Melodrama! Hysteria! He'll be ruined.

Not at all. He passed every dull GCSE.

He gets to the sixth form. He goes a bit existential and reads anything a bit French, sexy and incomprehensible and talks unutterable bollocks as teenage boys will.

For a while he reads only Kerouac or Rimbaud or Chuck Palahniuk. More condescending hysteria. Just wait! He's soon reading Fielding and Austen too. After 7 years here he's sane and scholarly and funny and easy with anyone. You cannot buy these things.

He shows me the letter.

It is an offer from Cambridge to read English.

"Cheers, Sir!"

I ring his mother. I thank her for sacrificing her son to those liberal principles and for never ever panicking. And for giving me a reason to be cheerful.

Spring in the step

Published 27 April 2006

Spring is all over the urban blight as I walk to school. I stand dazzled by daffodils and daisies. I wander still dazzled over the zebra crossing.

Crunch! Screech! A great truck shudders to a halt. The driver might not be best pleased.

"Oi!" he roars from his cabin. A tattooed trucker with a late Willie Nelson thatch.

I prepare an apology. "Oi! Sir! Hello, Sir!" he roars again. He seems pleased. Bystanders seem puzzled. Am I a lord? A peer of the realm?

"Wigwam! Don't you remember me?"

I can't recall a trucker from Texas over the last 30 years.

"Ben Levene!" he announces. "Erm" "You don't tho' do you?" "Erm."

"You were the best teacher I ever had!" So good I can't remember him.

Then it clicks. Ben. Ben Levene. Used to sit next to his chum Spud. Goths. Late Eighties. Skull earrings. Bright as a pin. Came to school on a Vespa. "The Hairdryer".

"Ben! Ben Levene! Hello!"

A Chelsea truck creeps up. "Do get a move on!" shrills a prune-faced woman.

Ben Levene. Often in my detentions. Used to sit at the back in media. Fixed the telly saved me from that inspector when it exploded must have left in '89 too cool for school.

We reminisce. Mrs Shrill honks. Another car creeps up. And another. They honk too.

"See! I done alright for myself in the end!" says Ben. Absolutely. The boy done well. From "The Hairdryer" to this 18 wheeler.

"Done your coursework yet?" We laugh.

Honk! Honk! go all the cars. "Fuck off!" goes Ben.

"Can't you see we havin' words! He's my old teacher!"

I nod. We reminisce further. "You still teachin'? 'Fraid so."

"You were tho'. The best." He's made my day. I tell him that. He releases the brakes. "Be lucky Sir!" "You too!"

The truck thunders down the North Pole Road. It hoots like a walrus. A tattooed arm waves the peace sign. I hope it's the peace sign. And Ben Levene is gone.

I am serially cursed by raging drivers. Who cares eh? The best teacher! I feel a bit smug and big headed and sentimental. I sit under cherry blossoms and have a Mr Chips moment. I ponder how important school is – and how it isn't.

He did do all right. Me too, apparently. I'd rather have the thumbs up from Ben than management. Sometimes teaching really is the best job. I wander up to school with a spring in my step. My pupils could be in for a treat. I just might be the best teacher they'll ever have.

Mentor and disciple

Published 14 September 2006

"Where's Crumlin?" I'm doing the 10th year register. Blank. One week in and he's out. Bunking. I'll have him. I launch into my annual motivational speech. The early season pep talk. I crank up the gravitas and machismo. I try to sound like Al Pacino or Sir Alex.

"Why's he talking funny?"

"Last year was easy this is the Big One 25 hours homework a week or mid table mediocrity no prisoners in Blair's Britain you don't want to end up drinking meths outside Mecca down the Grove we must compete with the spoiled darlings of the public schools time to get real it's a jungle out there!"

Dreadful guff. I can do this in my sleep. I seem to be doing it in theirs. They glaze over. We move to phase two. I dish out the thrilling AQA anthology and suggest they have brainstorms about Carol Ann Duffy. They go off into interactive differentiating empowering groups. The class purrs along at Ofsted level 1.

Enter Ronald Crumlin – the Prince of Darkness.

"You're late!" He's with a tiny cherub-faced boy in my 7th year.

"Why are you late Ronald?" "I'm a mentor sir"

"A what?" "A mentor. I'm showing him the ropes all week"

Ah. "I'm a guru. I'm a role model for the little 'uns!" Like the Artful Dodger. Or Nigel Molesworth. Or Mephistopheles.

"I'm orientating 'im. Miss Batty chose me."

"Why?" "I know things!" Like bunking and larking and dealing and making mischief.

"I'm going to be good this year! I'm going straight!" Several pigs fly over the science block. He introduces his young chum to our class.

"This is Walter! Little Walter!" "Hello Little Walter!"they say. Little Walter beams.

"And this is Wigwam!" I nod pastorally. Little Walter beams

"Hello little boy!" says Decibelle. "He's so sweet! Bless!" says Gina. Little Walter blushes at these trilling sirens. Crumlin is immune. "Can't hang about, sir!"

And they're gone. I see them throughout the day in the groves of academe. Little Walter hangs onto Crumlin's every word. Mentor and disciple. Sage and pupil. Pete and Dud.

I meet Crumlin after school. "Little fellah's well sorted. I gave 'im a piece of my mind" I shudder. "Which piece would that be?"

"Wisdom. Life skills, sir. He needs a mentor like me! Not any old muppet!"

Perhaps he's right. It's a jungle out there! Perhaps Crumlin is the best mentor any boy could get.

High G to low D

Published 5 October 2006

The Family Crumlin have been summoned to the school. They're waiting outside my room. I am Ronald's tutor. It is Assessment Review Day. He is a Special Case. Mrs Crumlin comes in with little daughter Alice and a baby in a pram. And the legend that is Ronald. He carries a ball in a bag and sits forlorn in a chair.

"Hello Mrs Crumlin!" We shake hands. I've known her for four years. She nearly smiles. She looks bone tired.

I gaze at the Assessments of Ronald. They are a catalogue of failure. Academic Doom. Ronald has been placed on a grid. The essence of Ronald Crumlin – citizen of King Hell Mansions – has been quite shrunk. He has been measured between levels 1.3 and 3.7. This is "interpreted" as a high G to a low D. In all subjects! Apart from football. He's on QPR's books – they too seem to be flirting with doom.

High G to low D! How would you feel? Ronald feels bad and gazes at his boots. Alice wonders if her brother is good. And Baby Crumlin squawks.

We survey the damage. We gaze at foggy jargon. Ronald is not meeting his targets. Well, me neither. Nor his mother I shouldn't wonder. It's a miracle she's here at all. Up since dawn to feed the children and take them to school and be an auxiliary nurse and then collect them and charge off to my school to listen to some lousy insults about her darling son. Again! She has tears in her eyes. I'm weary of being part of this.

Ronald, we read, must devise "strategies for improvement". He must write these down in triplicate.

What do you want him to say?

"I am rubbish!" It's a Laingian Doublebind. A self-reflecting hell. So he scribbles strategies.

1 - i must consentrate more

2 - i must not get led astray by Lunk.

3 - i must do 25 hores of homework and not call Mrs Batty a donut even tho she is.

I correct the spelling. Maybe he should have written the truth.

"You know and I know I won't change. I've had 10 years of failure and insult and bedlam. I am a Low F and I will wreak havoc forever."

He kicks the bag and looks at me like I've betrayed him.

I smile at Alice. "Your brother's good!" I tell her. Well, he is. Much better than a number on a database.

Mrs Crumlin shakes my hand. I tell her I like Ronald. She nearly smiles. She wheels out the baby Crumlin. Perhaps they could measure the little fellow on the way out.

Leaving it too late

Published 23 November 2006

Lateness week. I must come down like tons of bricks on the tardy. Even on my lovely 7th year. Even on Little Walter – still not much bigger than his briefcase – who has wandered in late to my lesson. He has missed my starter on the colon. I ask him for a late slip by the end of the lesson. And this is what he wrote...

"MY DAY SO FAR.
Alarm ring like heart attack. 'Get up!' yell mother. I snooze. 'Or you'll be late!' I snooze on. 'I'm not telling you again!' She have told me this umpteen times. Door slam. Off she go on early shift.

I wash and stagger into pale dawn (style eh sir?) for paper round pursued by killer dogs. Then eat organic gruel then pack sacks of homework and charge through Shepherds Bush and plunge into netherworld of tube and wait for Central line. Voice say 'Service as normal!' Pin stripe man say 'Oh fuck!' How we laugh! Other voice say 'Central Line is late ha ha!' Why? Who know eh? Bomb scares? Drunken drivers? Leaves on lines? Thames on fire? No! 'Insident on line!' (eufemisms eh sir!) We know what that mean! Another poor boy gone? Driven bonkers by curriculum. I sometimes contemplate it myself.

Train finally emerge. Throw self into crushed hordes. Train stop. Five million miles underground! Voice tell us we've stopped! Forever? Train start. Train stop. Then start. Disgorged at Notting Hill and meet Nigel at Burger King and nip down alley and get mugged by thugs who call us 'batty boys'. Bang go lunch money! Trudge on. Will we be late? (Suspense eh sir?) School gates clanking shut! We sneak in. We give IDs and fingerprints and DNAs to bouncers. What larks eh? Only one gauntlet to go! The Late Patrol They stand like vultures in foyer! Vholes and Batty and Mumps!

'Late!' say Vholes who look like Nosferatu.
'Late!' say Batty who look like thunder.
'Late!' say Mumps who look like parrot.
(Similes eh sir!)
'Late!' say mother who on mobile
Late! It will go on our files forever! We might never be employed!
'Death where is thy sting?' say Nigel philosofically. He is incarcerated.

I zoom breathless to your lesson sir. I am late because of tedious clots and fools who keep asking me why I am late! And that is my day so far. ps what use colons eh?"

Yours Walter."

I smile. I'm pleased he's out there. Dull it isn't. I write "Excellent –apart from dodgy spelling, rubbish verbs, and a rather crucial absence of colons!"

What can a poor boy do?

Published 1 February 2007

The Conservative Party's Social Justice Unit – aren't we flirting with the oxymoronic here? – has been considering the working classes. They find that they do rather badly at school. We know. They find that poor white boys get the worse deal. That only 24 per cent get A to Cs. Diagnoses are various. Absent fathers, macho sub-cultures, moronic infernos, hip hop music – and original sin. We've known this for yonks. And the remedy? Bigger funding and smaller classes and Tough Love. Fine. Simple. So do it. That would work for most.

But let's look behind these drear revelations – at just one of these folk devils. Let's look at Charlie "Hardcore" Johnstone. He's poor and white and 14. There he sits before me, concave of face and shorn of skull. His eyes are dead and he's shaking. So would you be if you were running drugs. Charlie has "gone". He's off the radar. He's seen off all support systems. And me. Especially me. I think I've got through to him – and then he hides in the giant flower pot in the staffroom. He's seen off the shrinks. Like Ms Limpet the Freudian who sits now in redundant intimacy next to him.

"Please sir, get her off my case – she's a mentalist!" he yells.

"And have we done our homework?" she chirps.

"Don't know about you miss, but I haven't."

No home.

Let's follow Charlie back to his home. Let's follow him through the dark wastes of Westway as he wanders through the bitter winds that blow around King Hell Mansions. There he goes past the incinerators and under the dark car park with its dead air and bent cans and needles and skinny girls who shiver and thugs who deal in menace and oblivion. Come on.

Keep going. Punch in the code and go down dark no man's land corridors and into the lift and up to the 17th floor to the triple locked door and into the tiny room where his mother is gaunt and pale and beaten and there's no books and no space to do our homework.

Charlie mutters and leaves to meet some thug. Or else. Or else he'll get something broken. Like a cheek bone. He sticks brute noise round his skull to kill the trauma of being Charlie "Hardcore" Johnstone. He is probably caught up in what psychotherapist Camilla Batmanghelidjh calls a "chemistry of terror"

"It drives you mental sir!"

No home, stupid. Nowhere to be still.

Contextual Value Added? Charlie should get an A* just for getting to my registration.

There he sits shaking and frightened and failing. What else can the poor boy do?

Different class?

Published 11 October 2007

The recent Sutton Trust report tells us that bright state pupils from poor backgrounds still find it hard to get into our elite universities. Pupils like Lily in my 11th year. She's just left some writing on my desk. A story. It is stunningly good. Imaginative, lucid, controlled. You can't teach this. You just recognise it and encourage it. Lily is very bright. Luminous even. I worry about her.

She lives off the Westway with her mother who's a nurse. They live in genteel decency in the brute inner city. Lily has always been a loner. You can see her in the corners of libraries or corridors or under the willows in the sixth form garden – with her pallid face and dark hair and fierce eyes. Reading. Always reading. Shutting out the busy world with a good book. She's just discovered Carson McCullers. She doesn't say much. Ms Limpet the Freudian felt compelled to Do Something about this. You're not allowed to be serene these days. Lily soon saw her off. Lily is tough. But tough enough to survive the antics of her less contemplative classmates?

They like her. "She deep, sir!"

"She dark!" "She genius!"

"She well clever!"

And she enjoys them. She relishes their wit.

But I still worry.

"Don't worry, sir!"

Even when Shaka's got his dreadlocks in the fan or Decibelle's at full throttle or Dillywig dangles from a window?

"Dull it isn't!"

She smiles. She waves. I hope she's waving not drowning.

"Chill, sir!" I try. But would she do better if she went to a private school – like St Custards down the road. Their pupils aren't lumbered with relentless testing and targets or the brute frolics of Sidney Lunk or the defenestrated Dillywig. Their pupils have small classes and huge resources and fluent cultural chatter – they can twitter with the tyranny of the articulate. Lily doesn't have their swaggering confidence and cultural nous – that seems to come with cash. And class. As *The Guardian*'s Jenni Russell says, "class is destiny". Still. It makes me want to hit things. There are lots of Lilys in our inner city classrooms.

I read her story. It seems even better. Different class.

Meanwhile I'll keep giving her the books. Flannery O'Connor next?

I hope Lily stays on into the sixth form. She's Oxbridge material. I can see her in those dreaming spires. I can see her with her books and fierce eyes in the shades of academe. She deserves them. And if those elite universities haven't got the suss to see these things, then perhaps they don't deserve her.

Lost in other worlds

Published 15 November 2007

I'm with the Top 8h year – always a delight. They're as clever as pins.

They stretch me. I must stretch them. With what? Let's see. Week 9. Lesson 29. "The Language of Persuasion." What? Again! Dear me! Off we go. I pretend to be interested. So do they. Except for one. Except for Walter. Little' Walter – moon of face with fog of curls. He's somewhere else. He's blithely reading a book. A sci-fi tome about time warps, astral projections and alien abductions from planet Zog. He's off, as ever, in a parallel universe. Off message. Off task. And, some keep telling me, off trolley. "We can't have this!" says Management. We must make "significant interventions".

So Miss Batty barks at him when he dreams. Mr Donut detains him when he doodles. Ms Limpet the Freudian sends him to the loony bin. We must rescue him from these alternate realities.

And get him back to this one. To noun clusters and conditionals.

Must we? I can't see a problem.

He's courteous and calm and terrifically clever and – apart from playing chess with Lily – a bit of a loner. He has lunch alone in the 6th form gardens. He walks down corridors alone with bulging satchel and Buddhist detachment. He's been sighted alone in the bandstand in Kensington Gardens lost in deep tomes and in other worlds. Gloriously immune to the inner city inferno, he seeks out solitude and silence. Gloriously immune to the clot curriculum, he seeks out deeper thrills. Like Mark Twain, he never seems to have let schooling interfere with his education. We can't have that! So we call him "eccentric". It's not difficult these days. He's quite brilliant so we call him bonkers. He might just be bored. He sometimes sighs at my more clanking disquisitions. He might just be a genius. I thought we're meant to be seeking that kind of thing.

Shall I get his attention? I seem to be quite peripheral to his intellectual development. Should I take it personally? Shouldn't I be fascinating him? Should I make a significant intervention? And confiscate the tome? Get him back on track?

He's not alone – half the class are somewhere else half the time. If I had their curriculum for 5 hours a day I'd be eating my head. I'd be negotiating alternate realities. Little Walter just spends more time there than most of us.

So. Shall I stop him? I muse.

"Why've you stopped, sir?" says the pedant Podge.

I was elsewhere. "Er … sorry"

"I'm lost!" says the industrious Emily.

Me too. In another world.

Kevin and the deadlines

Published 24 April 2008

Here comes "Little Kevin". There's a lot of him. Wide and round with spangled dreadlocks, he trundles down the corridor towards me. A less than Socratic dialogue looms. He owes me. English coursework. Management have urged a "final push" on exams. Sort of an Academic Stalingrad. Not easy with "Little Kevin". I've never "finally pushed" him anywhere.

He hails me.

"Alright then, sir?"

"No!"

"How's it going?"

"Badly! Where's that coursework!"

"Heh!' He does his Mafia shrug.

"Where is it?"

"Heh!" He's like an Italian defender on a red card.

"The deadline is April 24!" He doesn't do deadlines.

"Well? Have you done it?"

"Not as such, sir!"

"What as such?"

"Well... what it is... is..."

"What Kevin? What is it?"

"I got a lot on at the moment! As it 'appens!"

Like hanging out down Ladbroke Grove.

"I know you have! Your coursework! As it happens!"

"Chill, sir! It's on the way! No worries!"

"I am very worried Kevin!"

"Easy sir! Chill your beans!"

I have been chilling my beans for five whole years.

"Look!" I go pastoral. "It's alright for me! I've got my GCSEs!"

"Where it got you!"

Erm. Genteel poverty. Scapegoat of the ruling classes.

"A teacher! You the one with the worries! Know what I'm sayin'?"

"Look!" He goes philosophical. "We've always had a good understanding, right, sir?"

Have we?

"Don't spoil it, sir. Don't start being a teacher now, sir!"

Give me strength!

"I don't do homework. Never 'ave done. You know that!"

I'm breaking our code. I don't bother him. He doesn't bother me. I used to do the discipline. Detentions, ultimatums, threats. It didn't take. I rang home. I rang his mother, stepmother, sister, and dog. And once himself.

"'Little Kevin'? He not here!", said "Little Kevin".

It's time for some Zero Tolerance.

"Deadline! April 24! No excuses!" He's a borderline C. He needs his GCSEs. I must save him from those mean streets. "Five pieces! Right! Or..."

"Or what, sir?"

I'll lock him up 'til he does do it.

"Not gonna 'appen, sir!"

"Why?"

"You strikin' sir! April 24! Innit?"

"Little Kevin" trundles off whistling down the corridor.

Tuvshin wins again

Published 22 May 2008

Have you got a wind-up artist in your class? A pupil who gets to you and makes you lose it? I have. He's called Tuvshin – from Mongolia. He's in my 8th year. He has little English and a beatific smile. School seems to afford him much dark laughter – often at my expense.

We started off badly in September and it's just got worse. A connoisseur of mischief, he only gets on my nerves. I go haywire. I look like a boiling owl. He looks like a Zen monk. I drift into the personal, into Bad Practice. He wins. The larking never ends. He goes deaf at registration. He offers to read and he can't and talks in tongues. He puts Amy Supple's hair in an electric fan. He puts little Walter in a cupboard. He charms visiting management. The class find all this extremely satirical. He's up there with Oscar Wilde.

The girls find him sweet. "I could take 'im 'ome!" says Gina. I wish she would. And Miss Limpet the Freudian finds him fascinating. He is "ludic". Ah. "It's how he controls his world." And mine. We have a "disconnect". Not half.

Right. Next day I breeze into the classroom. I maintain a patient, patrician hauteur. It seems to work. We purr along towards Ofsted level 2. We zoom through Robert Swindell's *Abomination*. I smile professionally at Tuvshin. He is a model pupil. The lesson is exquisitely paced and timed. I move towards the plenary.

PIP! PIP! PIP!

A bit early? I check the classroom clock. It's conked out.

PIP! PIP! PIP!

I abandon plenary. I dismiss class. They pass by in creepy Trappist silence. "Thank you for the lesson!" trills Tuvshin. Ah, we're beginning to "connect".

Imogen Snowdrop remains.

"Please, sir... the lesson has not ended."

"I'm afraid it has, Imogen."

"No, sir! You've been duped, sir!"

"The pips have gone, Imogen!"

"I'm afraid they haven't sir! It's Tuvshin. He records them on his mobile. Then he plays them early. So we can leave early. There's 10 minutes left, sir!" Ah. "He does it in Mr Donut's lessons too." Ah. "I never told you this, sir!"

"No Imogen. Quite. Thank you!"

I peer grimly out of the window. My boys are doing high fives in the playground. Dervish is doing keepie uppies on the canteen roof. My girls are swooning over their darling Tuvshin. He smiles beatifically at them. He waves benignly at me.

PIP! PIP! PIP!

Has the lesson really ended this time? Or has the "ludic", larking Tuvshin returned? I'll have him. Next time it will get very personal...

The ghost of Charlie Johnstone

Published 29 January 2009

I'm walking down the dark streets of Ladbroke Grove. A keen Russian wind shivers my timbers. A thug swings a dog on a bit of wood. It shakes a traffic cone like a jugular. A fat black Cherokee truck purrs slowly past. A skinny wraith comes out of the shadows. It shuffles towards me in the hanging mist. It gets closer.

I know this face – concave and cropped.

It's Charlie Johnstone. I thought I'd never see him again. I was his tutor a year ago. A sweet, bright boy, he suddenly went off the radar. He looked all gaunt and sat at the back. Then he bunked. Then he got suspended. He was "externally included" or "internally excluded". He didn't know if he was coming or going. Then he was gone – thrown upon the mercies of the inner city streets. At fifteen.

He gets closer. A skull in the hanging mists. A spider tattoo crawls out of his jersey. Sleeves swallow his hands. He shivers. He holds a phone.

"I'm on it, bro!"

He clocks me clocking him. He tries to leg it. To be rid of me.

Like he tried to be rid of us all. Tutors. Shrinks. Do Gooders. The Old Bill. The whole caring crew.

"Hello Charlie!" He looks down.

"How's it going?" He tugs a sleeve.

"Er.. you know, sir." His face is quite cancelled.

"They put me with the fuckin' nutters!"

He means the Pupil Referral Unit in Colville Terrace.

"It's alright, considerin' "

He's got the shakes. He keeps coughing.

"I'm a good boy now!"

He nearly smiles.

"Might even come back, sir!"

"You should, Charlie. Dervish misses you. And Sabrina. We all do."

"Yeah! Whatever."

The phone chirps.

"Alright. Said I'm on it. Seen!"

He looks up and shrugs. Who was that? The social worker? His defeated mother? His guardian angel? Probably not. The phone chirps again. It's a text.

"Laters, sir. Gotta go! Brass monkeys!"

And off he goes. Past the square. Past the church – Our Lady of Walsingham. She shines in the falling night. "Pray for us all" it says. Not half. Especially for Charlie. I watch him disappear. To his home in King Hell Mansions? Or to his turf under the Westway? With the dealing and the damage and the menace? Who knows? Is he still running dodgy things to those rich folks on the hill? Notting Hill? Has the Street got him? I wish I could magic him away like the friend in 'Slumdog Millionaire'. Fat chance. He's gone. Quite gone. Charlie Johnstone slipping through the shadows. Slipping through it all. ..

That fat black truck comes back through the hanging mists.

Chapter 5

Testing and measuring the pupils

'This stuff drives you mental, sir!'

For many years teaching English was terrific. We could explore language and literature. There was choice. We could devise stuff for our pupils. It was called teaching the 'whole child'. Now we seem to measure it. Well, a bit of it? The complex fool that is Crumlin is a Measured Outcome. It started with the National Curriculum in 1988. If it moves, freeze it. Then test it. Then teach to the test. Informational retrieval. Tick boxes. Whoopee – exam results go up. Dumbed down. If you can't measure it you can't manage it, control it. Divide and rule and doomed. So we have the testing regime. Our mites are measured.

The most examined, most tested, and – most unhappy.

"Have I been streamed, sir?"

"What level am I?"

"Is this the thick class?"

"Is it cos I's stupid!"

"Have I failed, sir?"

Probably.

Look at their cancelled faces on Results Day.

Not at shrieking blondes in the *Daily Telegraph* waving their A*s in the sky. Look at the bewildered, cancelled faces cursing their Es and unclassified. And we wonder why they get a bit angry? A bit wretched? They've been deleted. The game is rigged.

We should be ashamed.

Of course we need some exams and assessment. But not this blizzard of testing.

I woz 'ere and I failed

Published 29 May 2003

I am sitting in a big hall under a big clock. I am the invigilator.

It's a Victorian workhouse out there.

They are having a test. Another one. I must send these tests to Mafia Exams Inc. I too must be tested – to test if my testing is testing enough. Professors can then test the effects of these tests. They pronounce them most malign and deleterious.

Tinies blub and gibber. Their secondary elders sweat and shrink and bunk. Sixth formers are punch drunk – by now they've had 150 hours of the stuff. They're the most tested tots in the world.

We don't teach anymore. We test.

"You may begin!" I drone.

Some zoom through model answers. Some just scribble anything fast. Others are mere cartoons of failure – there's the 'clueless but proud'. The 'rabbit in the headlights'. The 'search me guv' …

Half an hour in and lots are conking out.

I walk past faces once bonny and bright on that first day in big school. I could have told their grades even then. There's Dennis Plum – a nice round boy with nice round writing. Plum trades meticulously in the bleedin' obvious. He's been buried in an E grade all his life – it could well be on his gravestone.

There's Decibelle Cramp who still scribbles gibberish on texts she's never read. Felix Hercules has quite thrown in the towel. He is drawing a pigeon.

"Ere Sir – who's that stupid bro who gets shot?"

I move off with Zen gravitas. He completes the wings.

And there's Rhapsody Bland. Her Parker glides over the page in joined up thinking and perfect cadence…

We are moving towards the end. I still wander hatchet faced. The desks have the usual graffiti. "I woz 'ere and I failed," says one. It's Charlie Johnstone – caught in the fresh hell of another test.

He's blown the last 87 since reception class. I have rarely seen him so humiliated. How the mighty have fallen. A legend outside the classroom, Charlie wrestles vainly with yet more impertinent questions.

"'Sdrivin' me mental, Sir!"

Pencil in knuckle, he carves at the scars of graffiti. He's run out of language. He can't get loud or hit something or head bang it – or hide.

You don't want to look. He scribbles something. He covers it up. He gives me a wink. Then cancels his eyes and sits at his desk growing muscles. It's a massacre.

Charlie woz ere and he failed. He is unclassified.

Rhapsody effects a deft conclusion. She is an A*.

As we all well knew they would...

I look at the clock.

"Could you please stop writing now – it's time!"

To end these wretched tests.

When the Berlin wall came down

Published 20 November 2003

Before the wall came down I was a spy in the Eastern Bloc. A double agent in Berlin. I'm not sure for whom. I went with a busload of left wing loonies. A *Daily Mail* nightmare on wheels. It was called The London Communist Teachers Club. Our leader was Red Eileen from Acton.

We sped through the night to Check Point Charlie. Stern men with guns and no sense of humour shouted at us. I thought my head of department was a goner. Red Eileen soon sorted it. We were over the wall.

We spent the week incarcerated with the Stasi Ofsted in a big concrete block. The walls were festooned with paintings of kitsch Utopias. Maidens frolicked with hammers. Workers waved sickles. Stalin snogged tinies. "Work jolly hard and we'll succeed!" said the signs.

That nice Mr Honecker beamed at us too – just before he was done for fraud and corruption and multiple murders. Whey-faced men in dark suits droned on about pogroms and 5-year action plans and schemes of work. Good Soviet stuff. We asked questions about the schools.

Things were only perfect. There were no skivers, junkies, drunks, punks – or Charlie Nerks. Not in the Motherland. But each night on the streets we met skivers, junkies, drunks and punks in Pistols T-shirts. In the Motherland. I was stalked by the Stasi for smuggling Kafka to our gorgeous interpreter. What thrills!

We visited schools. We walked through hushed aisles of toiling pupils. All on message and ticking boxes. They were lovely and literate and smiling. They sang sunny songs to us. Just like my Cubs' Gleeclub. They gave us teddy bears. It was impressive – and heartbreaking. I wanted to believe in it. But it gave me the creeps.

Then the wall came down. It all went west.

These days I'm still a bit undercover in the free west. Men in dark suits gaze upon aisles of toiling pupils. I am one of these men. The tots tick boxes. They are having a baseline test. A test by which other tests can be tested according to a 5-year plan.

An air hostess voice squeaks disembodied through speakers. "Start!" "Stop!" "Go!" "Turn over!" "In HB pencil only!" "Two minutes left!" "The end!"

Not half.

Then a grim man gives tots a spelling test.

"And! To! It!" he barks.

Charlie Nerk and Attila Dervish click fingers and thumbs. No probs!

"Door!"

Most tots in comfort zone.

"Receive!"

Erk! Nerk and Dervish on the ropes. Dennis Plum quite done for. "Pusillanimous … vicissitude … "

Most tots quite crushed.

"Malfeasance."

Indeed! Nerk and Dervish do fuck-off faces. The test ends. The computer sheets are sent to Durham. Or is it Berlin? Tots exit. In silence I walk down the corridors. Past the signs for Utopias. "Work jolly hard and you'll succeed."

It's efficient – and heartbreaking. And it gives me the creeps.

Coarse work time

Published 26 May 2005

Our deadline for the GCSE English coursework was last July. Most did it. Rather well. Some didn't. At all. We know who they are.

Crumlin, Dillywig, Lunk, The Mooch and Decibelle. The usual suspects. And even Gina.

"You'll fail the exam! You won't be entered." They'll fail if they are entered.

"Whatever!" The final ultimatum shifts to September.

September arrives. Coursework doesn't. I thunder ultimatums.

"December – Judgement day!"

December arrives. Coursework doesn't.

"Need more time!" says Crumlin.

"You! Dillywig! Done it?"

"Not as such, Sir!"

"Deci?"

"No point Sir! You know I'm an F!"

Our last final total utter ultimatum shifts to March.

"You're only 43 weeks late!"

March arrives. Coursework doesn't. I lock them all up in cell block 101 – for three whole evenings.

"Against the rules, Sir!"

"I don't need exams, Sir!" mutters Mooch, "my brother can get me a job."

"Yes you do!" I yell sulphurously. I bang on with the usual guff.

"Get real … Blair's Britain … essential skills … jungle out there. You'll thank me for this!" I bribe them with doughnuts and fizzy drinks. I dish out panic worksheets for all occasions. "Romeo and Juliet – Fate or Freewill?". "Sherlock Holmes – Genius or Junkie?", "Eddie Carbone – Hero or Clot?", "Shrek – Cool or What?". Key quotes, bullet points and conclusions. "Just give the examiners what they want! Five bleedin' pieces!"

They scribble and scrawl and curse and crank them out. They hand them in. I mark them. They're mostly dire.

Except for the original writing. Fantastic stuff. Tales of fear and loathing in the inner-city. Lunk goes for the confessional mode. I hope the exam board doesn't send it to the Notting Hill Nick.

The Mooch oeuvre is so street it's lost on me and the examiners unless they're hip to Ladbroke Grove argot. He doesn't do full stops. Not one. Crumlin writes a heartbreaking yarn about dogs dying in lifts in a spider scrawl and with car crash spelling. Real, raw, lost voices. They will fail. Dodgy grammar and you're finished. Decibelle is right. I've always known she's an F.

Gina is the exception. She's A*. A revelation. She hardly speaks. She mostly bunks. She's a writer. Night falls. They shuffle out.

"Well done! One day you'll thank me for this!"

Will they?

"Whatever, Sir!"

Well … Gina might.

Teaching to the test

Published 15 June 2006

England will win the world cup. They've got that whizzo midfield. David Cameron will become PM. He's got the moves. And this year's exam results will be the best ever. They've got the answers.

You just know. Some things are easy to predict. Like exam grades. Even in my subject – English.

It goes something like this.

Government set up grim exams. Mafia Exams Inc have the contract on the knowledge. Edexcel, AQA, OCR – they're all at it. Chief examiner is the Godfather.

He set it. He mark it. He know answers. His answers. He write crib for his exam. He in cahoots with publishers.

Pearson, Heinemann, Hodder Murray. They're all at it. We must buy crib. We must deliver the knowledge.

Pupils must buy crib. And cram 'til blue in face. It all go back to Mafia. Mafia mark it. Godfather tick it. They go laughing to bank. Pupils do better than ever.

School zoom up tables. We keep job. Management give themselves pay rise and BMWs. Man from ministry look smug and wear halo. Man from Ofsted he say "satis". PM smile brightly.

The Spectator lament Mickey Mouse exams and compare them all to "Dunciad". *Daily Mail* agree – and has leaping A* blondes on cover.

And CBI will yell at spelling and pronounce end of civilisation. What larks eh? What a racket!

We may as well be doing golf course maintenance – in all subjects.

It bores us dumb and the pupils dumber. I can see them now in the exam hall. There they sit in the hum of the air conditioning. Knocking out the knowledge. Scribbling for their little lives. And ours.

Go drudges go!

This afternoon it's English A level. I must check the paper. I construct a happy face.

Zen calm. I zoom in – like a hangman. I unwrap it. I check questions. Yes! Perfect! Just as I predicted. We've been doing them forever. We've covered them.

Lock stock and module. My class will be alight. I give them my Zen gaze and skip back to staffroom and do the Crouch. This robot stuff is all the go.

Outrageous? Depressing? Absolutely. Most teachers think so. Most writers too. The society of authors says that targeting textbooks at exams kills learning.

Philip Pullman says it's just "teaching to the test". It's robotic. Sue Palmer thinks it immoral.

"The more you focus on exams the less well you teach." Twas ever thus – but never this bad.

But what can we do? Mafia Exams rule.

Mafia exams plc

Published 3 May 2007

Exams loom. Out goes education. In comes parrot learning. Teachers zoom around waving crib sheets, boosting D grades, shifting deadlines and cursing clots who leave coursework on the Circle Line.

Like football managers, we're only as good as our last results. I'm lucky. I don't have an exam class. But I must prepare my English set for next summer. They need all the help they can get. Then I see a headline.

"MARKERS SELL EXAM TIPS!"

Senior examiners are holding seminars telling teachers "how to beat the system". So says Warwick Mansell in *Education by Numbers*.

Crumbs! "We guarantee the best grades for everyone!" says big chief. Crikey! In most subjects! Like French? Orals? They'll sell you the questions! All 42 of them.

Schools call these tips the children's "burglar bill swag bag". "Children like this idea of stealing!" says big Gallic cheese.

Like History. They'll also flog you questions – at £200 a go. "This is realpolitik – ends justify means!' says big historical cheese. Crikey! I better get real. I better pop along to one of these cheating seminars

Off I go down the mean streets of west London. I go down the Portobello. I nip down dark alleys. I see a door. "Mafia Exams", it says. I press a bell. I see a hatcheck girl. "I'm Mandy." she purrs. "AQA. English. Fly me." I give her a coat and a smile and a pony and I'm in.

She takes me to a dark room. A chief examiner sits massaging league tables and a cat. He's got a head like a peeled egg and swivel eyes and a sign on a desk. "BA Cantab", it lies. "What you got?" "What you want?

Original writing? We got three writing frames and five headings and 10 bullet points! We got adjectives to turn Ds into Cs. Cost yer a monkey!" "Literature?" "The lot! A* stuff!" "Romeo and Juliet?" He breathes in like cowboy plumber. "Do yer act three, scene five six headings and eight paragraphs and 22 potential essay starters!" "Like what?" "Like, 'Juliet's duologue with her mother is full of dramatic irony, such as'." He strokes the cat. "Such as what?" "That's another pony!" "And poetry?" "That's top whack! Duffy don't come cheap. And that Plath's a grand. Miserable bitch. Can't see it myself!"

"Anything for my EFG grades?" That's half my class. "For the pondlife! Nah! Do what most schools do, leave 'em to the streets!" My pupils? Plum and Lunk and Crumlin? Never! They're better than this craven stuff. And much more honest. I make my excuses and leave.

It's research, innit!?

Published 5 July 2007
"A searing indictment of utilitarian philosophy," concludes the clot Dervish of *Hard Times* in a coursework essay.

Dear me. There's more

"I have never read a more burning denunciation of the dismal science of classical economic theory. Not for sale in Canada."

Jesus wept. He's not alone peddling this gibberish. Shaka too is tremendously awed by literature.

"We can but admire the rich metaphorical resonance of his cymbals," he scribbles. Indeed. And I can but admire his gall. I blame the teacher.

That would be me. Can it get any worse? I'm afraid it can. Here comes Plum: "This play explores a dizzy existential abess!"

Not half Dennis.

I ask him to read it out loud. He does. It's like swallowing marbles.

"It's plagiarism!" sighs Cordelia Swansong.

"Thank you!" says the blushing Plum. Any ism is alright by him.

"It's cheating! You nicked it!"

"It's research innit!"

"You don't even know what existential means!" trills Swansong.

Plum crushed. I collect it. Tear it. Bin it. "We could all end up in the slammer!"

There is, apparently, a lot of this about – from utterbollox.com who peddle parrot answers at £100 a go. Wretched stuff. What has spawned it? Bad exams and the tyranny of tests. A utilitarian philosophy even. Teachers lose their nerve and pupils lose their voice. I've had enough. So have the QCA. They've just decreed that coursework will stop. They will ban it in many subjects. There will be "controlled assessment" instead. Whatever that might be.

What a shame! Any English teacher can spot and stop plagiarism. If you can't you shouldn't be teaching.

Coursework should be kept. It should be the best part of the course. It's about flair and finding your voice. The old AQA A level lit did just that. It really let them loose. It really trusted teachers. There were no suffocating targets. Our pupils were free to do creative responses or pastiches or essays on "Tom Waits and Flannery O'Connor" or "Jim Thompson and Jacobean Tragedy". Thrilling stuff.

Off we'd go with bagfuls of brilliance to see chief examiner Buckroyd. Assessment was a real pleasure. I've never seen better work. They meant it. They had their own voices.

Like Plum does sometimes. "Lady Macbeth can't hack it and goes doolaly," he observes. That's more like it! Go Dennis! Right answer. Wrong register. But it is his! And probably a searing indictment of utilitarian philosophy.

Mock markings

Published 15 January 2008

I'm giving back the English mocks to my 11th year. Once again I've had to mark the mites. Are they quaking in their boots? Not at all. They've been marked since birth. What's another test? Another dreary definition? They've got exam fatigue.

"Pressure! Pressure! Pressure!" go staff briefings.

"Work! Work! Work!" go assembly mantras.

"It could drive you mental, sir!" says Crumlin, whose psychic good health has always hinged on deep sloth.

Mine gets more fragile. I get angry that pupils become mere grades. They're shrunk to smithereens. Just like my lovely subject English.

Still, I make with same old motivational address. They've heard it all before. Some mock yawn. Some join in.

"Jungle out there... work rate..." drones Dillywig.

"Perspiration not inspiration... prisoners not taken" chirps Shaka

"Didn't get where you are today without hard graft eh, sir?"

Well, yes as it happens.

Teacher. Marker. Wicked Messenger.

I give out the papers littered with red ink. Some flinch with failure. Some punch the air. Some shrug stoically.

"Fair cop, sir!" says Crumlin gazing at another D.

They've done rather well, actually. This parrot learning is paying off.

There's of lots of high grades. Sophie Garnish and Lily are A*s. Dragana and Cleopatra sparkle. The girls have all bounced up their grades. The boys less so. But they've given it a real go.

Dillywig's piece on London at night is in the James Ellroy mode. It has vigour, narrative pace and graphic violence – "then I saw off his head".

Crumlin displays similar energy, crap spelling, grocers' plurals, functional illiteracy – and street poetry.

"Street lites were like helloes". Go Ronald! Dull he isn't.

Plum is. As ditchwater. I bounce him up to a D. He beams.

Lunk still displays very dim inklings of Duffy's rhetorical strategies.

"This Duffer poem is so intresting," he scrawls.

"It's not though innit!" He winks. He doesn't really trouble the scorer.

Nor, I'm afraid, do the Estonians – Miftar and Milhaljo – what with no English. Shaka merely free associates – what with the skunk. And Charlie is absent – what with the drug running. He went AWOL over Christmas and his mum hasn't seen him since.

Still, it's a great team performance. Our best yet.

"Well done! We're getting there!"

They seem quite unmarked by it all.

Speaking and listening

Published 1 May 2008

I pass along the corridors and catch snatches of the pupils' speech. It fizzes with quick wit and street rhythm. A rich west London vernacular extremely fit for purpose. Unlettered and unfettered and unexamined. A shame. I wish we could use it for the Speaking and Listening GCSE coursework. I've just done the final marks for this, my favourite exam. It acknowledges the pupils' lives and voices. They do well. They'd do even better if it celebrated the vernacular. They must be more formal. More pompous. More middle class. They must argue, formulate, chair debates, and use the "grammar of spoken standard English".

Of course. "And communicate with different audiences."

Different from the Grove posse.

Fair enough. But spontaneity can get snuffed. Some just lose their voice. And such critical vigour seems rather superfluous for some pupils' speech. It's a sledgehammer on a nut. Like Dennis Plum's on fishing. Plum is a what-it-says-on-the-tin sort of fellow. He showed us PowerPoint pictures of Kensal Green Canal. Click!

"That is a bream! That's a gudgeon!" Click! "That's a perch! That's an eel!" Click! Click! There were lots more fishes. "Any questions?"

"Yes. Do fish feel pain?" said wet Rhapsody.

"How would I know?"

Plum just didn't tick the boxes.

Rhapsody did. She spoke most trenchantly on "Why I am a vegan".

"You kill animals and they'll kill you!"

"What! No bacon sarnies?" said chairman Dervish.

Shaka on Rastafarianism and Heavy Dub – and possibly skunk – was mesmerising. He delivered his ruminations in a patois of Jamaican/Grove/Moon language and at times trespassed into the criminal. Should I have shopped him to the local constabulary? His argument was foggy, his sense of audience negligible and his grammar non-standard. He would have given Melanie Phillips nightmares. So I gave him an A*.

Sidney Lunk on hara-kiri – with illustrations – gave us all a turn for the worse. Not easy with a working vocabulary of a teapot. His listening skills were also duff. Electing himself mute didn't help his cause.

"I's listening!" he said grabbing his ears. "What else is I doing?" Should I have given him an A* for role-playing an idiot?

They ranged loosely over many topics. Arranged marriages, Lebanese cooking, Sudanese wars, Franz Kafka and much more. They were never dull. They were pretty good. But not as good as that real vibrant stuff I caught along the corridors...

Mrs Schofield's GCSE

Published 18 September 2008

"Today I am going to kill something. Anything."

The 11th year are transfixed. Even the more distrait. Even Decibelle. Especially Shaka. "Wha' appen?"

I continue. "I squash a fly."

"Chill, sir!"

He can chill. He hasn't yet clocked that I'm reading a poem from the AQA GCSE Anthology. "I pour the goldfish down the bog."

I do my Dr Lecter voice.

"The budgie is panicking."

Some laugh. Nervously.

"There is nothing left to kill."

"It's like Eminem!" says Shaka. It's not. It's a Carol Ann Duffy poem – Education for Leisure. I go on.

"I get our bread knife and go out."

The class are mesmerised.

"The pavements glitter suddenly." Brilliant line. I pause.

"I touch your arm."

And then? Who knows? That's it. The end. There's a stunned silence. Chilling indeed. A tense, dangerous poem. A shocking insight into incipient psychosis. Like Eminem. Like Snoop in The Wire. The class get it. They know about rage and alienation and bad education. They talk of "shivs" and "shanks" and "nutters with knives" in the shadows of the Westway. We discuss context, form, language, irony and the dramatic monologue. I tell them about Genesis and King Lear. They tell me about Eminem and Grandmaster Flash. This poem has always prompted terrific lessons...

Not any more it won't. It's been banned. We must "destroy the snthology" say AQA officials. Why? It might prompt copycat killings. Lethal misreadings. Who says? External examiner Pat Schofield.

"It's absolutely horrendous – what sort of message is that to give kids?" It's not a message. It's a poem. Complex. Rich. Difficult. She wouldn't know a poem if it bit her on the bum.

Why do AQA listen to these twerps? What's the next text for the knife? Duffy's Stealing? About another nutter? Cut! Or that other GCSE favourite Macbeth? Knife crime? You want knife crime?

"He unseamed him from the knave to the chaps!"

Cut! Cut! Shaka might start chopping up his budgie! As if. How depressing. How patronising. Why don't they trust teachers with texts? It's what we do. This is the triumph of the philistine. Of the stupid. It makes you give up. You feel like killing things. Like goldfish. Or external examiners.

But, wait, all's not lost. Carol Ann Duffy has replied with a poem – Mrs Schofield's GCSE. A withering and witty poem.

Poetry triumphs over the philistine. Imagination over dullness. Excellent!

Chapter 6

Testing and measuring the teachers

'You have only met 29 and a half targets!'

Testing times for teachers too. We must be tested to test that our testing is testing enough. So we must teach to the test so that tots pass their test and we pass our test. These are testing times. You're like a football manager. You're only as good as your last game. Your last SATs. And the last SATS was gibberish. And lost in the post. Hurrah!

Who does the testing? Ofsted of course on a 'lightning strike.

They zoom in with their grim clipboards. You trot out the model OFSTED 1-2-3 lesson, give them a million schemes of work and leg it. Who manages the testing? Leadership Management Groups. Who they? Heads as they used to be known. I've worked with some cracking heads. Intellectuals. Socialists. Delegators. Bruisers. All quite different. All terrific. All let us be. Let us teach our subject.

Then. Wallop! Modern management moved in. It's easy to demonise management. So here we go. They're like estate agents. 'Vholes, Mumps, Batty and Dazzle and Fizz'. They don't teach. They manage. Schmooze and finesse. Divide and rule. It's all spin and suits and tufty haircuts and mission statements. They glare at us at grim briefings. The Reservoir Clots. They speak in cant. Aspirational bollox. It's plastered all over the walls.

'You can't trample infidels when you're a tortoise!' Eh?

'Life is a rainbow which also includes black'

This is where language goes to die. Miss Mumps of Line Management tells me I've not met my trillion targets. Met them?! I wouldn't recognise one if it bit my bum. They want to control and cull and cleanse the school of its infinite variety. They rather did for us woolly ditherers, us old-fashioned, decent liberal wafflers. They're everywhere. This is the New World Order.

Why looking daft does wonders for the mind

Published 10 April 2003

Like many schools, we're having a makeover. This involves a compulsory dress code. After 30 years of free expression my pupils are to be decked out in a uniform. It comes in rather fetching shades of grey. It is casual and cool and tinies can still sport the designer hoodlum look – all hooded and hip like Eminem.

This is a big mistake. The whole point of a uniform is to look daft. Academic success is consequent on a hideous wardrobe.

Take my old school – the Royal Grammar School, High Wycombe. We were top of the league. And why? School uniform. Our dress code was flannels and short trousers, sensible footwear and garrotting ties – and a cap perched like a golf divot on the knotgrass hair. You couldn't be seen in public. You had to hide in libraries going blind over Gallic wars or pluperfect tenses or Marianne Faithful.

This was essentially the Nigel Molesworth look. The local girls school sported the Nigella Molesworth – ditto with kilt. Both ensembles promoted a pallid and hectic erudition. We were on cerebral heat. Some of us had to be incarcerated in 'The Express Class' until we squeaked with opinion of the type rewarded by exam boards. I became a bit of an expert on sexual delirium in Racine. At 13.

No boy in his right mind wanted to look like this. A few broke the code. They were deemed 'wide boys'. They looked cool, like Elvis or Jerry Lee – and not like Clement Attlee. They wore drainpipes and Brylcream and creepers. They hung out in Mac's Cafe listening to the Shangri-Las when they should have been in the library conjugating irregular verbs. They attracted cool girls with candy-floss hair and pencil skirts, which played merry hell with their irregular verbs. They got low grades.

So if you're going to have a uniform, you've got to go the whole hog. It should be strictly hideous. It should reflect the present craze for streaming and measuring and labelling. The gifted and talented should sport kilts and the odd woggle. This should keep them cerebrally occupied. The not transparently talented should adopt flannel, ties and the odd boater. Nutters and disruptives could simply wander the corridors in dunce's hats. There should be lots of shorts.

That should do it. Out with the cool. In with the daft. My pupils will be forced to skulk in libraries and condemned to find the national curriculum interesting.

Their levels will zoom up. I will, at last, be deemed competent. And we'll be a beacon school bouncing to the top of the tables.

Battle for the books

Published 5 February 2004

Our English office has had a makeover.

We've been hot desked and no shelved. And no booked. It hurts. It's all the go. Our books have all gone. Our lovely ramshackle office has gone too.

It used to be full of the moribund, crumbling and fuddy duddy – and the books weren't much better. It used to hum with laughter. Now it just hums with gizmos.

Now we must have blue sky thoughts on pine top tables. We're surrounded by shiny surfaces and gun metal cabinets and a colossal absence of books.

Books are out. Technology's in.

Our government is mad for it. They spend zillions on it. £25 million on interactive whiteboards. And 0.4% of the school budget on books.

Schools everywhere are invited to buy whizzo software. We can acquire Macromedia Studio for 'only £2199.' Or a Promethean Collaborative Classroom which facilitates remote communication activity through ACTIVslate and ACTIVote – what we teachers call 'talking'.

Or we may care to relish the Intellitools Classroom Suite – "the ultimate teaching resource," says Trish Hornsey. I will just "love these cross curricular authoring tools" – or 'pens' Trish …

Ofsted too is mad for it – for PowerPoints and wireless networks. Its reports mention technology seven times more than books. Schools spend three times more on it than books. Children learn much less from it than from books. Half of key stage 3 pupils don't have books. Meanwhile roofs leak. Classes get too big. Books disappear.

Ours seem to have been consigned to storerooms and boiler rooms. We must save them. We lug them down corridors and into car boots. We are caught in the techno gaze of CCTV as we cart the canon away from a place of learning.

Our sixth form library, too, has shrunk. It used to be an ivy-strewn beech wood sanctuary of twilight contemplation. It tumbled with tomes ancient and modern. They're giving them away. There's Orwell – surely never more relevant?

And what's this? Boswell's *Life of Johnson*. The greatest biography in the English language. A must in any library. No matter that it's not read. If you won't read you may as well not read something good. And they've kept the biographies of Posh and Becks ...

There's nothing wrong with fancy software – but not at the expense of books – or Samuel Johnson. I must rescue him. Shall I put the good doctor in my classroom? No chance. No shelves. Shall I put him on top of the whiteboard? An inspiration to us all! An old musty fat book.

I half expect the great Cham of Literature to come thundering in and whack a few machines to smithereens with his dictionary.

All tied up with red tape

Published 4 March 2004

Primary teachers don't much like those national curriculum tests. But they didn't boycott them. They panicked – and kept them. They felt "nervous" and "insecure". They craved the safety net of SATs and all those tidy schemes of work.

It's all about fear, says Philip Pullman. "The national curriculum has put a cage on everyone."

On secondary teachers too. They too don't like the tests but there's still no boycott. They still seem to need a big brother curriculum which requires that we churn out endless schemes of work. They've got us by the modules. Lock stock and learning outcomes. So we map and model and sequence things. Not for ourselves – but for Mr Ofsted.

"Where's your scheme of work for week three module two?" he quizzes keenly.

"There!" we'll smugly drone, "I have just fulfilled assessment objective 17 of *Stig of the Dump*!"

"Well done! Have a pay rise."

He buzzes off – to return in 2 days.

"Where's learning outcome 13a – eh? Eh? Gotcha!"

So we're all busy scheming. I must deliver virtual lessons to my virtual charges. But I'm not Postman Pat nor are pupils passive vessels. They're Charlie and Shaka and Dervish and Rhapsody – a richer mix you could not find. They are beyond most schemes of work. It's like nailing jelly to the ceiling.

"And key stage 4?" I drone out scheming model answers to my punch drunk 11th years as they apply mascara and lipstick and try to stay awake. Surely we don't have to knock out these schemes at key stage 5? Apparently so. I ride roughshod over literature with brute simplicities.

I knock out drear and withering schemes on *Wuthering Heights*. I trash John Donne. The Ecstasy? Does it celebrate – (a) the body (b) the soul (c) neither or (d) both? Tick a box. Teachers still feel "nervous" and "insecure" without this. They panic and doubt. Donne celebrated panic and doubt – reading his stuff is a nervy two-way thing. A bit like teaching a class.

There's nothing wrong with planning. I don't want to go back to those door-knob lessons where I didn't always find out what I was teaching until I heard what I said. Mind you they were interactive. And you could take risks. And the pupils did so much better.

We nearly knew what we were doing. I didn't want more. We did not need schemes of work.

As Tim Brighouse said at the time: "We do not need a national curriculum because we've already got one."

I've still got that one in my head. A richer mix than all this scheming. I want it back. I want to be trusted.

But I'm not. You're not. Teachers are not.

As Philip Pullman said recently: "They're nagged, they're controlled, they're harassed. Set them free!"

New age mumbo jumbo

Published 5 May 2005

This is a bonkers time of year. It's all coursework and SATs and deadlines and targets to fail. I get stressed. I go to the doctor. She goes new age on me. She gives me a tome of new age therapies.

Feng shui, left nostril lunar breathing, creative visualisation, primal screaming, astral planing and Phyllis Krystal's wave imagery are just some of them.

I must listen to the chirping of birds in the boughs. I must get some red and orange flowers. They reduce crime. And deep music will massage my brain.

This stuff is everywhere. Mumbo jumbo. It will heal many things.

Do you fidget and twitch? Are you distracted, disorganised or dyslexic? Or raving and all a-twitter?

Are you thinking what I'm thinking?

It's my eighth year! Last lesson on a wet Thursday. Here they come stampeding down the corridors. Jolly thumping flagellants. Distracted and raving and very much a-twitter. Seventeen of them are SEN. And there's no support teachers.

Shall I go new age on them? Shall I go holistic not ballistic?

I make a tape. Monks and madrigals and whales mating and Albinoni and Alice Coltrane and flute music of the Andes ...

I unleash it on the class. Most are entranced. I point at the red and orange flowers on my desk. "You like this shit, Sir?"

I am unruffled.

"Can I put Snoopy Doggy Dogg on?"

No. I turn off the tape. There is silence.

"I want you to put your heads on the desk and close your eyes."

Most do. Dillywig puts his in the desk.

"I want you to do absolutely nothing."

"No change there, then!" whispers Rhapsody.

"I want you to listen to the silence!"

We search for our inner child. Crumlin searches for his inner thug. He does a lot of yelling. "He's having a laugh."

Then he shuts it. Silence. A tiny peace in their little lives. Shhhh.

"Erk!" yells Decibelle. She's always favoured primal screaming.

"I want you to imagine you're somewhere else," I drone organically.

"Where are you, Dillywig?"

"Burger King, Sir!"

"Can you all hear the birds chirping in the boughs?"

I hope my teacher chums don't come in. There is a cathedral silence. There is no mother-cussin-penlosing-tellhimsir-you'regay-yourmum'saprossi-youcouldn'taffordheranyway discourse

They listen carefully to something or other – entranced by mumbo jumbo ... As if.

My so-called support

Published 12 May 2005

My department is under rolling observation. It's called support. It's relentless – even though our results are the best in the school. My chums are barking and beta blockered.

We need support for this support. I need paramedics in the playground. I've been on the rescue remedy for weeks. I've got another class observation tomorrow. A merry crew – often troubled, lost, war-torn – they're as sharp as pins and mad as hatters.

We muddle along. It's a delicate and nuanced negotiation. It's taken two terms. We now learn things – although not always on the Ofsted model.

I'll do my party piece: *Dracula* – the simile and metaphor lesson. Never fails …

Enter Mr Vholes our inquisitor. "Don't mind me," he whispers. He sits next to Sissy Jupe.

"Oi Sir, 'is 'ead's on the wrong way!" she observes. Mr Vholes is bald and has a beard.

I zip through the register. I do the requisite starter. We're off. We gaze at overhead projections. We gaze at an extract of Nosferatu. They are mesmerised by the visage of the vampire. I solicit similes from the class. They're on my side. They chirp poetically across the room.

"His eyes are like …"

"Lizards, sharks, hooks, echoes, gobstoppers, ciggies that have gone out …"

"Excellent!" Are you listening Andrew Motion?

"Like glowing jewels embroidered across the sable night," offers Rhapsody.

Precious – but Mr Vholes must be purring.

His head is like … ?

"A billiard ball, a shrunken peanut, brackets, moonbones, a bleedin' egg – your mum …"

Similes rain down like government targets. I put them on the board – their rich wordhoard.

Well done my little chums! Pick the bones out of that Mr Vholes!

He does – with some relish at our debriefing. I am apparently not quite "satis". He blethers on about interaction, expectation, differentiation and hierarchical discrimination.

"Boy looking out of window – boy chewing – girl with hand not up – Plum insufficiently stretched – daydreaming girl off message." Dragana? She's Albanian. She's traumatised by wars.

The rich mix of the class seems quite lost in the brute gaze of Mr Vholes.

He's back the next week. I'm back on the rescue remedy. I must do robot formal lesson. I never teach like this. Class are bewildered. I yell at them. Some yell back. I yell louder.

Our delicate rapport is blitzed. My tiny chums feel betrayed. So do I. By the uncomprehending and relentless Mr Vholes.

Open evening fibs

Published 20 October 2005

I'm looking unusually fetching in my M&S suit from their rather modish Autograph range. I've gone for that David Miliband look – a sort of oleaginous spiv number.

It is open evening. We must spin the place like billyho to the well heeled of Kensington. I've been tramping down Portobello market with a placard.

"Bring us your band one Tots. No more the nutters! Don't send them to St Custards or St Trinians – send them to us!"

The school has had a makeover. The gardens have morphed into Kew. Flora and fauna have been suddenly magicked like Gatsby's parties.

Tommy the caretaker has hoovered every falling leaf and twig and crisp and condom. The foyer looks cutting edge – like a Nip and Tuck clinic. Plasma screens blink, desert plants bloom, silver fountains play and clocks tell the time in Tokyo and New York and Shepherd's Bush.

Delightful tots usher parents to whizzo displays and glitzy shows. Trim teachers schmooze them down spotless corridors and glowing walls.

Where's Crumlin and Lunk and Dillywig? Airbrushed. Off limits. One look at that crew and we won't get Cordelia and Marigold.

The school is bereft also of the more unsightly and less spinnable teachers.

Where's Mr Trauma of drama with his earrings? Mr Grumps of media with his tattoos? Grimes of science with his ZZ Top beard? And the pedant dotards of the English team? We've been consigned to the crepuscular shades of room 101 with dictionaries and classics and some rather good exam results.

We plan to enact *The Ancient Mariner* but we have no punters. Despite our suits and roses, we blush unseen in murk.

Pip! Pip! The main event! A phalanx of Milibands and Milibandesses. PowerPoint images of charming multi-cultural Tots.

A light falls on a lectern. A keynote speech!

The school is a passionate caring palace of modern excellence. We're zooming up league tables like Chelsea. Teachers are a mix of Mother Theresa and Plato and Jamie Oliver, constantly seeking genius.

Designer fibs. Schools have to do this. It might even be half true. But our school is better than this. Richer. It's like that Labour conference. I feel a bit bilious. I feel a Walter Wolfgang moment coming on. I long for the ghost of Nigel Molesworth on that PowerPoint.

He hav a message for all parents.

"Any skool is a bit of a shambles, as you will discover soon enough"

Not meeting the targets

Published 16 November 2006

I saunter grimly towards the management suite nerve centre. I've been given a window by line management for our weekly pedagogical tryst. I must meet her to measure the targets I'm not meeting. I say good morning to the Kosovan woman tweaking litter under the equal ops poster and cross hushed carpets to the door. It is open. Management has an open door policy – this promotes a more interactive human resource space.

"Do come in!" trills management behind a clump of cacti. I enter a windowless and bookless room and sink into a sofa. She has a rictus smile behind the desert foliage. There's a bulletin on her desk with the "word power" theme of the week.

"Lie on your back. Look up at the sky and discuss whether it was made or just happened."

We seem to be in David Icke territory. Computers breathe. She cancels a smile and fondles a mouse and glares at a screen. "You have presently 29 targets!" Click!

"You have met three of them!" Is this good?

"You have half-met five of them!" Click!

"You have, therefore, not met 23 and a half targets!"

Met them? I'm not on nodding terms. I'd say hello if I could fathom what they were. She scrolls through blizzards of failure.

"Collation of strategies for twilight synoptic workshop."

"No evidence!" Click!

"Peer group criteria awareness initiatives!" Click!

"No evidence!" Click!

"ALIS database grade predictors grid audit tracker graphs positive residuals"

Moon language. Bats speak this stuff. "No evidence!" Click!

"Exemplar schemes of work and modules on *The Ancient Mariner*."

"No evidence!"

But my pupils all got As! I sink deeper into the sofa. I feel like *The Ancient Mariner*. She drones on. I feel rage. I can't express it – because I bunked the assertiveness training workshop.

Thirty years at this lark. I must be good at some of it. But all I do is fail targets. My whole department just fails targets – 377 at the last count. Their exam results are terrific. Most are passionate, decent if battered old lags. Followers of Empson and Leavis – and Molesworth. Literature is hugely important to them. They're like Hector in *The History Boys*. They're "passing it on". If they go, it all goes.

She gives me a window for next week. I shuffle out. I smile at the cleaner. I bet she's failing targets. I see Crumlin sitting on a football. He rolls it to me. I whack it like Gerrard. It nearly decapitates Dillywig.

"Goal!" At least I'm on target!

Passing it on

Published 23 October 2008

I'm at a meeting of English teachers. "Recent Initiatives at A Level". The pulses quicken.

We're getting orientated. We're getting professionally developed. And terribly bored. I settle down for a decent snooze. But wait a minute! Who's that over there? Two alumni – from 10 years ago. Old Girls. Kate and Bianca. Feisty intellectuals. Bright as pins. A level pupils. And now they're teachers. We wave across the room.

"Hi! Sir!"

"Hello Miss!"

We hear of "new exciting ways to read a text".

They seem very similar to the old dull ones.

We hear about "new assessment objectives".

Tedious imperatives. Drear impositions. My goodness, this lark has got so prescriptive. You can't wing it anymore. Did I have assessment objectives when I taught them? Not as such. I'd breeze in and be a bit random and anecdotal.

"You get paid for this, sir?"

Well, yes. Badly. But yes.

I really liked that class. And our set texts. Except for The Taming of the Shrew. Blue murder. Never got the plot. Still don't. Kate elucidated it with a brilliant cartoon map – still used by some of London's more expensive schools. And John Donne could get a bit tricky. Bianca helped me out with the more arcane and filthy passages. They did jolly well and now they're fabulous teachers.

Against the odds. Against a lot of modern nonsense.

"Education models itself on crap 80s TV shows!" Well, yes.

"You have to sell your soul a bit, otherwise you'd spend your whole time grumbling."

A raving old dotard, I do rather a lot of the latter.

They are judged and performance managed. Remorselessly. By clots and philistine fools. Their lessons are deemed "unsatisfactory" if 10 per cent of the pupils are not "engaged". What? Three! Out of 30? I've not done that in 30 years.

And they must work from dawn to dusk. Can I get them a drink? No. They can't stay. It's "Marking Review Week". Last week was "Book Check Week". And before that "Observation Week". And before that "Senior Leadership Observation Week". They come round on "Learning Walks" with the dread clipboards "identifying failure".

Next week is "Mock Ofsted Week". And the next one is the real one. Dear me. I thought I had it bad. Why can't they be left alone? Trusted? Set free? They'll just burn out. We'll lose them. It's a wonder they don't go half daft. It's a wonder they're so good.

They teach English with a Leavisite zeal. They're passing it on. It's all you can do. They're tough and fast and funny and inner city sussed. They're gold dust. Like so many young teachers. Heroes – and heroines – of this tawdry age.

The disappeared

Published 2 April 2009

A fading photo falls from an old register. Easter 1987.

Who are these alien, smiling people? The Grateful Dead? The Amish? Bolshevicks? Out patients from a Bin? No. The English Department BNC – before the National Curriculum. A happy shambles. Variously gifted, but always most serious about teaching and literature. Leavisite, socialist, idealist, a bit silly. All gone.

Wha' 'appen?

They were 'disappeared'. Culled in the culture wars of the noughties. The school was 'turned round' – from a sixties liberal folly to a modern exam factory. You know how it goes. You need the following.

A new demon super head who is visionary and inspirational – like Putin. New Labour apparatchiks who deliver the McCurriculum. A Leadership Group who point their power suits at you in grim Briefings and threaten you with ultimatums in a soft and verbless purr. Much flash refurbishment. A foyer which resembles a City consultancy with cut hyacinths and retro chic sofas and drizzling water features and smiling receptionists who look like Stepford wives. The walls too must be festooned with feelgood, fortune cookie cant.

Then comes the culling of the teachers.

Which teachers? 'Bad teachers!' says Michael Gove.

'I will break them!' said the demon head.

Cripes! How many? About a hundred. In about 18 months. All rubbish? By what criteria? Off message? Off trolley? Wrong haircut? Wrong culture? A loathing of that wretched testing? Or a member of the NUT? All were. Who knows? Too glamorous? Too old? Or perhaps too unsightly? Beyond spin, they were banned on parents' evenings.

The Fear was everywhere.

Someone was always 'failing' something. They were inspected to destruction by consultants with enough criteria to sink Socrates – usually with floridly bonkers 8th years in stifling tiny rooms. Until they conked out and were put on 'capabilities'. Until they got sick and took to beta-blockers or booze or blood pressure pills. Management had them by the modules. They were dead meat. Their desk was cleared and they never happened – after 20/30 years. They had done the state some service. No matter. They were bullied, bought out, gagged and replaced by 24-year-old acolytes. Who cared? No one. The NUT was summoned. Big guns. To no avail.

Thus was the school 'turned round'. Like many others. It zoomed up league table. Those meretricious league tables. The new teachers are terrific, hugely professional and must work like billyho to 'compete in the global marketplace'. Dear me, it's grim. Corporate culture rules! Some look like bankers. Some are bankers. I don't envy them. Little freedom. Little control. No union. And not a lot of smiling. Unlike my long lost – and sorely traduced- chums of Easters long ago.

Chapter 7

Government wheezes

'Every Child Matters'

Tweedledee and Tweedledum. National Curriculum. The government's big wheeze. 1988. Since then they've hatched blizzards of them. Edicts and Improving schemes and ultimatums and initiatives, initiatives, initiatives. I've seen them all off.

Baker, Blunkett and Balls and the legendary Ruth 'Zero Tolerance' Kelly. Dear me. I don't control who I teach, what I teach, where I teach or how I teach. I must deliver their curriculum.

And not just the curriculum.

Social stuff. The 'broken society'.

Our fault. They tell us what to do. They've got a lot of Czars.

Obesity Czars, Anorexia Czars, Dyslexia Czars, Drug Czars, Respect Czars, Literacy Czars, Porn Czars, Culture Czars, Turkey Twizzler Czars, Smoking Czars, Gun Czars, Knife Czars, Manners Czars, Foreplay Czars, Condom Czars, Synthetic Phonics Czars, Exercise Czars, Litter Czars, – and Melanie Philips. They've got a lot of experts. Can I be one? PhDs in the bleedin' obvious. Bearded fellows from top universities spend years researching. They find things. Like …the poor don't do very well. The working classes have a tough old time, boys are violent and can't read books, girls are good talkers, synthetic phonics are the answer are not the answer are bollocks. The cane is bad for you. Boundaries are good for you, subject knowledge helps, drugs are rubbish and the rich succeed and SATs are rubbish the poor don't and rain falls downwards and the Tories will win the election and Cordelia Swansong will go to Oxbridge and Ronald Crumlin won't and Charlie Johnstone will go mad. We know. We've always known. Then they send in Ofsted to check. A Kafkaesque world where 'satis 'means 'unsatis' and 'good' means 'not good' and 'capabilities' means 'incapabilities'.

We pay these things no heed. We plough grimly on.

Like Grendel's mum – Ofsted returns

Published 24 April 2003

They're coming back – like Grendel's Mum (the monster from the epic poem Beowulf). The Dread Ofsted. What do they want this time? Can't they get a proper job? Like teaching? Teachers are conking out. It's all that pressure – like Ofsted.

I've been done four times. Surely I've seen them off.

But this time it's tougher. Young Dave Miliband is smokin' out the elderly and failing. That's me that is. Must prepare. I brief the class on how to conduct themselves should Joseph Stalin wander in. We don't want a repeat of last time.

"'Ere. Sir. Is he a copper then?"

"She's well fit!"

I must be seen to deliver the Ofsted Model Lesson and nothing else. The old one-two-three. It must go thus …

ONE: The Start. Class salute on entry and sit down in Trappist silence. I define learning targets. I unleash literacy scheme. Today we are doing the colon. I am pacy and perky.

TWO: The Middle. This will be active, pro-active and pan-active and chock full of finely differentiated meta-cognitive hierarchical interrogation and Socratic dialogue. I enact the fashionable jargon. We are all on task, track, speed, stream, message. I interact and differentiate like billyho.

THREE: The End. The plenary. I tell the class with luminous clarity what we have learned. I dismiss them. They leave cerebrally enhanced, salute Joe Stalin and observe most audibly their teacher's ability to render even the dull numinous.

Meanwhile in the real world it goes …

ONE: The Start. The class enter shambolically. I beg them to divest themselves of hats, hoods, gum, plugs, mobiles and lollipops. Classroom resembles a car boot sale. I float some musings concerning the colon. Class less than riveted. Joseph Stalin gives thousand mile stare.

TWO: The middle. I am conducting a soliloquy at a car boot sale. Some of class are more errant than interactive. Charlie zooms around the room like a helicopter. Differentiation is minimal and dialogue very fleeting. Most pupils off message, stream, target. Nigel out of the window. Me off my rocker. Lesson conducted in a cold sweat.

THREE: The Plenary. I announce to any pupil kind enough to listen that our Learning Experience could well be terminating. I remind the class what we may have learned – and of what we could have learned in another school with another teacher. The class shuffle out.

"Don't fancy your chances, Sir."

I then dismiss them.

Man from Ofsted – Joseph Stalin, still with the stare – says "Rubbish!"

Wot I want is knowlege

Published 8 May 2003

OFFHEAD REPORT ON MY TEECHER BY ME NIGEL MOLESWORTH – SUBJET Knowlege

Lamentible – hav he red anything in last 500 years? he seme to kno only two books. we hav done "Mise and Men" for last trillion lesons. it go on and on interminally. "George I want ketchup" he sa in a voice like a clot. Wot about some-thing relevent eh? Hav he not red my own work in Pinguin Twentieth Century classics?

Only other thing he hav read is ted Hugh and his peom Hork Roasting. Eyes go blodshot and he rave like loony. It is ful of entrales and blud and goor. It make wets feint.

The NASHUNAL KURRICULUM is a foreign countree for him. Does he kno his levls? Does he kno his YELLIS from his ALICE? Eh? A shambles.

LITERASY SKEME hav he heard of this I arsk myself. Is it a coma or a semi coma he below at us in hase of alcohol – DOES HE NOT KNO? One boy sa Yes! one sa No! Clots wave slates in all directions like flag of surender. Molesworth 2 havn't a clue. He even arsk me. Peason hav slate upside down. Then fule drop it.

next week he takle apostraphy. It is a wonder I stil knowe my grammer backwards.

CLASSROOM CONTROL ho ho. Minimal – It is not a lerning environment. He shout a lot to no avale. When he lose temper it is Enos effect. Teecher need to come down on us like ton of bricks. Any fule kno.

DRESS CODE Some days he look like something cat hav brort in. Other days he try to look like Tony Soprano. The felow need consistensy.

DIFERENTSHUN Point to answer! he yell at Peason. Clot can't point to own head. He hav the SPESHUL NEEDS. I lose wil to live and file nails. Teecher spend to long with Clots and hav no time for Us Gifted hem hem.

SUMING UP he hav let himself go. it is trajic. This is electronic age he belong to quil. Wot must he think when he gase out of window during millionth reading of "MISE". am I casting purls before swine? Could I hav been foopball star or peot or made something of myself?

BUT NO MATER!!!! In concussion I say KEEP HIM ON! We mite not learn Nashunal Kurrikulum. SO WHAT? we lern life. We hav a larf. KEEP HIM ON. otherwise weeds in shiny suits will make our tiny lives hell and ful of targets.

I Diskard them all. above teecher is briliant. We need the old Pendant. He hav tort me all I kno

is sumery alrite? leave 50quid at bikeshed !!! signed by me. N Molesworth

With apologies to Molesworth by Geoffrey Willans – Penguin Twentieth Century Classics

How low can you go?

Published 24 February 2005

Did you see the last Arsenal v Man U game? Wayne Rooney swore every 3 seconds – often at the referee. The referee could do nothing. Couldn't even give the spudfaced nipper a yellow card.

I sometimes feel like that referee – especially with Dave O'Hooligan. Look at him! He's doing a Rooney. He too is swearing incontinently. I too can do nothing. He's on a yellow for serious misdemeanours. It makes no difference.

There are Rooneys all over the nation's classrooms. I need help. I need some advice from our leaders. "Any poor behaviour is too much and should not be tolerated!" says Ruth Kelly.

I must write this down. Why did no one tell me this before?

But I'm always not tolerating them! They just don't seem to clock my intolerance.

"Exercise zero tolerance!" pronounces La Kelly.

If only! I'd put all Rooneys in stocks in the foyer. Tiny seventh years could pelt them with rotten fruit. But I'm not allowed to do these things. It doesn't, apparently, play well on parents evenings.

How much zero does she want?

I must learn about modern behaviour modification. I pop along to the Zero Tolerance Workshop.

"Set limits! Set boundaries! Carry out threats!" scrawls a consultant at a PowerPoint. Flippin' heck! We do role play. We practise the Alex Ferguson hairdryer rant and the Roy Keane stare. We rehearse the Clint Eastwood silence. We learn about 'turnaround schools'. We do not learn about poverty, despair and alienation.

OK I'm ready. Bring 'em on! I will unleash the whole repertoire on the 10th year. Where's Dave? He's doing a full Rooney – level 10. He's swearing once every 2 seconds. I apply the zero tolerance.

"I will not tolerate this poor behaviour!" The class are aghast. I reinforce boundaries like billy-o.

"Do you feel lucky, David?" I do the Clint silence.

"Desist David! Or it's the bootcamp!" I do the Roy Keane stare.

Dave O'Hooligan is like a lamb.

"Cripes, Sir! I have been hitherto most remiss!"

"I'm exercising zero tolerance David!"

"I know Sir. Strewth! It don't half work, Sir! Where did you get this concept from, Sir?"

"Government initiative, David! Now get on with your noun clusters!"

"Yes sir! Three bags full, Sir! Thanks for setting such clear limits! I'm so sorry for past misdemeanours Sir!'

Easy peasy! Thank you Ruth.

Classes need to shrink

Published 3 March 2005

In 1967 I was teaching 10D *Of Mice and Men*. The room was tiny. The class was large – nearly 30. Boys hit each other and girls felt sorry for Lennie. We muddled along. But I wanted a smaller class.

Somehow I passed. I got a postgraduate certificate in education. I got the badge. It has counted for nought. Since then, someone somewhere has forever been telling me how to do it.

I've been advised and badgered and hectored by consultants and cabbies and inspectors and ministers and managers.

I've attended a million workshops with grumpy frumps with sugar paper or sleek experts with PowerPoints, all talking mumbo jumbo about assertive discipline and control modification.

It didn't help.

Ofsted want the whizzo robot lesson. I must do snappy starters and pregnant plenaries and model and scaffold and "orchestrate a range of strategies including inferential and evaluative skills". I must "consolidate" and be "inclusive and ambitious" and pro-active and interactive and hyperactive.

And differentiate like billy-o. With 30 pupils – and no support?

It doesn't help.

How must I teach English? With traditional grammar. No! It kills creativity. Transformational grammar. No! Look and say? No! Phonetics!

Or semiotics or semantics or synchronic structures or Chomsky's universal grammar. I've ploughed through Vygotsky and Piaget and Skinner and Bloomfield and Bernstein and his restricted codes.

Rivetting stuff. And now we're back again to traditional grammar. We're back to the literacy scheme.

"It doesn't help!" says Philip Pullman. "It doesn't work!" says York University. I must now use "synthetic phonetics". Who they?

After 35 years at the chalkface I know the only thing that works - however you teach.

Small classes! No more than 10 pupils.

It's 2005 and I'm still teaching 10D *Of Mice and Men*. The class is large. Thirty pupils and still no support! The room – 101 – is even tinier. The windows can barely be opened so no one can flee the national curriculum.

In winter, the pipes make the room fetid. We need fans. In summer the heat makes the room fetid. We have fans everywhere. Shaka got his dreadlocks caught in one and Decibelle lost some tresses. And Crumlin shredded Dennis Plum's coursework.

"It was a U grade, Sir!"

We're all jammed in and get cabin fever. I don't want smaller classrooms. I just want smaller classes.

So double the teachers! Double their wages! It's so obvious. And it works.

Special measures

Published 1 March 2007

I'm being inspected with my not-top 8th year. The disappeared. The forgotten. It's where you go if your levels are low and you're poor. There's 10 SENs and 15 EALs – and no support teachers. I do the safe lesson on similes.

"Were we good sir?" "Jolly good!" Duller than usual but they think good is acquiescent. "Satis!" pronounces Inspector Vholes. Hurrah.

But "satis" means "unsatis". Oh. Is I rubbish? I mention the inner city context. I tell him this isn't St Paul's.

"Same criteria applies," drones Vholes. I tell him he's a clot and to stop bashing comprehensives.

Like Pimlico school they've just been put on special measures.

My daughter was a pupil there. Some of her friends went to St Paul's. St Paul's did "better" than Pimlico. Well, yes they only take alpha girls. But why bash Pimlico who take all god's children? My daughter loved it. She did alright. So did her chums – the Pimlico girls. They still talk fondly of Mr Lewis and Mr Bagan and headteacher Mr Barnard who crossed the playground just to say good luck to my sometimes turbulent daughter.

The staff worked permanently against all odds. The school was an architect's folly – boiling in summer and freezing in winter – with crumbling walls, tiny libraries, English in the canteen, and no stage for Ms Simpson and the best drama department in London.

And always the wonderful, liberal and battered staff dealt patiently with pupils from the poorest parts of London. Slap bang in the richest part. And with never ever any support from the Tory council of Westminster. Just negligence. Especially when run by Dame Shirley Porter who was done for massive fraud and flogged "homes for votes" rather than give money to the community comprehensive. Pimlico still succeeded.

My nephew's now there. He likes it. He's doing alright. Despite the crumbling classrooms, which flooded last week. Despite the lack of money. A levels results are still good. GCSEs too.

"Key stage 3 students are not making enough progress," bleats Ofsted. Just like my 8th years. Another failing school. Mr Barnard is bullied out. After 30 years. There's a farewell service with the lovely Pimlico choir. He has done the state some service.

We know what will happen. A tough new head to "turn it round". Governers sacked. Staff gagged. Children streamed. Parents spun. And the soul of the school quite lost. I feel angry. My daughter more so. "What! Lovely Mr Bernard! He saved my life!" She might have to get the girls round. The Pimlico girls.

Keeping it real

Published 15 March 2007

Did you see that photo of Mr Cameron and the hoodie? A real belter. Iconic even. Our future prime minister walks away from a sink estate. Ryan the villain stalks him. "He's behind you!" The villain mimes gunshot. "Click, bang!" goes the horrid hoodie. "Bang! Bang!" goes the Cameron cool. "Oh dear!" goes the spin doctor.

It's a real Little England. The Aristo and the Asbo. Lord Snooty and the Bash Street Kid. Dave keeping it real. Ryan keeping it ugly. "I was doing it for a laugh," says Ryan. Well, I'm afraid he's succeeded. It prompts much mirth in me. And easy, facile responses. Irresistible parallels.

Dave from all that wealth and Eton and Oxford. Ryan from all that poverty and a sink comp and King Hell Mansions. One from the Bullingdon Club –for Oxford's toff elite. The other from the "Benchill Mad Dogs" – for Manchester's hoodrats. The Bullingdon Boys famous for booze and drugs and trashing things. It's called hi jinks! Ditto The Mad Dog Boys. Asbo stuff! It's called delinquency. And Mr Cameron - the Caring Compassionate Conservative on a mission to understand these maniacs. I even feel for Mr Cameron. I often feel like Mr Cameron. Any inner city teacher does. I meet Ryan the hoodie – everyday. I know him. Here's in my 10th year. He's called Sidney Lunk or "Big Ant" Furnace or poor Charlie Johnstone. Wind up artists. Wise guys all. Clever in all the wrong ways. They keep me honest. They keep me sharp. And, I'm afraid, they keep me laughing. Darkly – like that dreadful Tony Soprano. There I am on playground duty I spy my boys. Shuffling and hooded and hiding behind the bike sheds. I wander towards them – in a caring, compassionate conservative Cameron sort of way. They divest themselves of smokes, phones, drugs and probably even weapons.

"Good morning boys!" I say. "Hey blood!" they chirp. Blood? Is that good? Is that friendly? We exchange pleasantries – about QPR or coursework or their frolics in Mr Donut's lessons. I feel rather smug. Cool even. I seem to have a rather enviable rapport with these hoodlums. They promise to be good boys. "It's all cool, sir!" I walk away. They go "click bang," with their hands and wave V signs behind me and knife Mr Donut's tyres and get sent home and come back and look contrite and promise me things and I nearly believe them and then they do weed or worse and then burn the bike sheds. They've got me beat. Again.

"We've got to understand the roots of crime!" says Mr Cameron.

Yo! Dave!

Get rid of 'em all!

Published 22 November 2007

"They're out there again, sir!" yells Sidney Lunk. "North playground, sir!" Sidney is our spy. "Shall I tell 'em to fuck off, sir?" "Er, no thank you Sidney!" "Who is it this time? The Obesity Police?" "Nah!" "The Drug Police?" "Nah!" I sigh. "I wish they'd leave you all alone!"

"I think it's you they're after, sir!" I ditch the conditionals and gaze out of our window. A black van purrs. A siren howls. Red lights flicker. "Taylor and Woodhead Plc," it says. "Culling and Capabilities – Sack 'em in Seconds."

"Don't fancy your chances, sir!" Two grim figures sit in flickering lights.

"Who's that one?" "Cyril. Sir Cyril to you Sidney." Sir Cyril Taylor – big government guru.

"Who's the other one? Looks like a pillock. With a hedgehog on his head?" "That would be Chris Woodhead." For it is he! Woodentop! Former Education Czar. I thought he'd been put out to pasture. I thought Ted Wragg had seen him off!

"What do they want?" To sack teachers – 17,000 of them! "Poor" teachers. Wrong 'uns.

"Get the wrong people off the bus and the right people on!"

What bus? Where do they get this number? Am I a wrong 'un? It's so easy to think you're rubbish. To be disappeared. We lost a few last week. What was wrong? Who knows? Perhaps they were bit left? A bit NUT. A bit old? A bit principled? A bit battered? How was it done?

You give them huge classes in tiny rooms – full of damaged loonies.

Then you fail them because it's not like Roedean. Ms Morris, the best history teacher in London, went thus, weeping.

"They're getting out, sir!" Headlights are doused. Two figures cross the playground. "Coming our way, sir." I go back to conditionals. "You gone a bit pale, sir!"

"Right! Model behaviour! Or else!" I remind them I've a wife and daughters to support. That Christmas is coming. "How much is it worth then, sir!?"

I remind them that I'm marking their mocks. "That's blackmail, sir!" "Quite!"

"Sometimes you are a bit rubbish, sir!"

"Not always though, innit!"

"He's alright, considerin," says Plum – who will get an A* for his mock. Click! Click! The footsteps get closer!!

"You want me to deck 'em, sir!" "No thank you, Sidney."

Knock! Knock! Door creaks open. They creak in. Woodentop first! Class sit silent. Pins drop loudly. Brilliant discipline! What Good Practice!

"Why's he got a hedgehog on his 'ed!" says Sidney Lunk.

Oh dear! It's the poorhouse this Christmas!

Get cultured boy!

Published 6 March 2008

Another central directive! "Culture for all pupils!" So say Ministers Balls and Burnham. "Culture enriches lives!" And so it does. It will be "top quality", "world class", "avant-garde", and "cutting edge"! Hurrah! We'll be "the world's creative hub"! Strewth! We'll be creating like billyho.

"Five hours a week!" No less. No more. I thought we did this already. It's called English teaching. Culture is central. Not peripheral. Now it seems to be a compulsory enrichment programme. All a bit Stalinist. Like my old teacher "Chunk" Jones.

"Get cultured boy!" he barked. I was 15. He was mad.

It sounded painful. Like circumcision.

"You don't want to be a vegetable do you?"

Well... "Or a wide boy?" Well… yes actually. I was rather partial to low culture. Like the sexy "Ronettes" or Wee Willy Harris.

"Chunk" was peddling High Culture. The posh patrician improving stuff. It rarely took. The poor man tried. He dragged us off to Francis Bacon in the Tate. We felt ill. Or to Bach cantatas in the Wigmore Hall. We felt bored. Brian Rumble fled. And once to an opera in a church hall. Huge bosomed ladies bellowed at us while starving in attics.

It got worse. We went to a French classical tragedy. Great Greek warriors were enacted by tiny French dwarves scantily clad in washing up cloth. They couldn't lift their swords or their corpulent girlfriends. The heroine's suicide had us howling with mirth. Then our hero dropped her and lugged her off stage right. We nearly died laughing. "Chunk" stopped the show and apologised for our barbarian insensitivities – and gave us the biggest bollocking of our lives.

Now I must be like "Chunk" and get my lot cultured.

It sometimes takes. We've been to La Haine and Baz Luhrmann and listened to Simon Armitage. All terrific. But often it doesn't take…

The fringe *Hamlet* – sometimes bollock naked – provoked giggles. Ronald Crumlin just said "No" to Noh Theatre. The Bulgarian modern dance troupe with concrete music was always ill-advised. And avant-garde theatre fell flat with my boys. I met Sidney Lunk at the interval. Or "half-time" as he calls it.

"Can't do any more of this! Driving me mental!"

I send him back in. "Jesus, sir. I'd rather be watching QPR!" But he must get cultured. "You too, eh sir?"

Erm…

Of course "culture for all" is a Good Thing. Central.

We could do it properly if they junked the national curriculum.

It can only get better

Published 17 April 2008

"Alright for you teachers! Twelve weeks' holidays a year – dossing!" So says a righteous business clot. Not half!

This hols I've done nothing but doss. I lie around in hammocks sipping wine under blossoms.

"Hello birds! Hello flowers!" I go.

I feel blissed out. A bit bipolar. Why? Pondering on Things Educational.

I glance at teachers' blogs. They're like sites for Samaritans. I glance at newspapers. Our children are the saddest, most violent, most bored on the planet. Seventy Cambridge academics have just published 23 reports on the last 40 years of education.

It's rubbish, they conclude. "It's utterly failed!" Blimey! "Real learning has been fatally abandoned!" – for pointless testing. We know. You didn't listen.

It can't get any worse. Well, it can. In secondary schools. They've reached tipping point. Me too.

I glance at the Easter conferences. There are some fantastic turns – like minister Jim Knight. "Big class good! Small class bad!" says sunny Jim. He will "allow 70 pupils a class". Go Jim!

It gets better! Here come Big Ed Balls. He'll also "allow" me to do things. To search pupils for "weapons, drugs and stolen goods!" – like airport security. Big Ed has torrid *Daily Mail* visions of my inner city pupils. I have visions too. I imagine them trudging in after the hols…

"Line up! Line up!" I curb foaming bloodhounds.

Pupils charge in like buffalo hungry for exam success.

Except for Sidney Lunk and Attila Dervish. They are devoured by dogs. Only bones remain. "Easy sir!"

I zoom round room with metal detector. "Big Ant" Furnace goes off like a fire alarm. I flush out daggers, swords and the odd Kalashnikov.

"I got rights!"

"Not any more you haven't!" I DNA the wretch. I advance on the quaking Shaka. I flush out skunk and condoms.

"It's my religion, sir!"

Who's next? Plum! Dennis Plum! Plump Plum is fleeced of pies. Poor Rhapsody's in tears. Bloodhounds sink their gnashers on her A* essay on the ambiguities of Armitage.

Now I can start the lesson. I start the Starter. Pip! Pip!

The lesson ends. Things are so daft you just laugh.

It can't get worse. It can only get better. I see the green shoots of revolution. Teachers call a strike – and not just for the money. They've had enough of all this rubbish. They seem to be standing up for themselves.

I'll drink to that!

Are we coasting sir?

Published 27 November 2008

"Are we coasting, sir?" says Little Kevin from his lookout by the curtains.

Probably.

"Is that good, sir?"

It's about as good as I get.

I've been in school since dawn. I've marked 60 books, knocked out 20 reports and some UCAS References. I've checked out Midyis scores, predicted exam grades, planned mock "Mock" papers, finessed a few figures for ASDAN, and rehearsed Luke for his Cambridge interview.

I've phoned Charlie Johnson's mum about the court case and Dave Mania's dad about the crowbar and the swans, and seen Lily's shrink in inclusion. I've lost the will to live in a staff briefing, and met Ms Mumps to fail some nasty targets.

I've stopped a punch-up in the dinner queue and smoking in the toilets. I've taught John Donne to the 7th year and some manners to the 8th year, and the alphabet to seekers of asylum, and read that something called Civitas thinks that Ofsted is something like bollocks.

It wears you out. I slump on desk and peer at the 9th year. At least there's no SATs. I can go through motions. Oh no I can't! Kevin is still yelling. "They're out there, sir! In a van. Big Ed Balls' mob!" Which one this time? The Fat Police, the Food Police, the Phonics Mob, the Drug Czars?

"NO! COASTING COPS!"

Who they? Another government edict! We can't "coast". "Satis" is now rubbish. I must "stretch" the little mites even more. Look at them. Most are at best "coasting". Some are in the doldrums. Moose and Chanteuse are becalmed at Level 2. Attila is listing. Finbar is in the shallows. Skint has sunk. Dervish walked the intellectual plank long ago.

And Little Kevin? He seems to have gone into the Bermuda Triangle of Academe. "Coasting"? He's been coasting since conception.

Most teachers are as knackered as I am. It's week 12! It's the inner city! What's wrong with a bit of coasting? A bit of creative indolence?

"They're coming our way, sir!" yells Little Kevin.

Quick! Bang up some "Aims and Intentions". Any aims. Look up the Levels! Any levels. Turn on the PowerPoint. Let's get interactive! Bang! Bang! They charge in with their culling eyes and clipboards.

We do "Conspicuous Toil"! A well-honed routine for these eventualities. Fantastic! Check that low hum of Socratic dialogue! The low purr of intellectual curiosity...

"We ain't coastin, we just chillin," says Little Kevin. A distinction lost on those clipboard cops.

Who cares? They're gone. I slump back on my desk. "Carry on!" What a breeze this inner city teaching is.

Chapter 8

Two nations

'It's another world out there, Sir!'

I bike to school every morning through the streets of London. Through wealth beyond the dreams of avarice and poverty beyond the nightmares of most of us. I pass swish palaces and gated communities and exclusive lawns – and King Hell Mansions and ruined communities and travellers by fires under the Westway. Two nations. I'm passed by roaring Chelsea tractors. They ferry their offspring to St Custards or St Cakes – to any school where my pupils aren't. Their tots perch in smoky windows and peer at my passing oinks.

'Fuck off posh gits!' say my charges, tucking into a breakfast of Coke and crisps.

London's been streamed. Just like our school.

It's about 60%:40%. Teach to the tests and finesse a few figures and you'll get your 60% GCSEs passes. The rest can go hang. They can go 'unclassified'. They can join the 'underclass'. What words. Like Dennis Plum. Or the dread Lunk. And Charlie Johnstone can get lost with the dogs of Westway…

The gap widens. It's like the fifties! The 1850s. Read Mayhew. Read Dickens. 'Little Jo' in *Bleak House* has not gone. He's alive and unwell and illiterate.

"I don't know nuffink!"

He can't read the signs. He seeks asylum. Just like Jiri who can't read the signs of the underground. Miss Batty tells him he's late. The wastes of 'Tom-All-Alones' have not gone. Look! That's Charlie Johnstone shivering under the Westway! That's Charlie flogging 'charlie' to the darlings of Notting Hill. It's like an American city – like something from 'The Wire'.*

Not every child seems to matter.

* Scrap all twilight workshops and watch 'The Wire'.

How the other half live

Published 22 April 2004

I pedal through gridlocks to morning school. The streets become chock full of children. They pop up from tubes and tumble off buses and kerbs.

Hooded boys do wheelies or thump each other and yell "Your mum!" Tenth year girls apply mascara and lipgloss and yell "Nice bike, Sir!" They're like a jolly invading army.

Other children move in the opposite direction. Tots in shorts and boaters and woolly caps and bobble hats and plus fours. They are escorted by grave parents who scythe blithely through my antic hordes.

They too are going to school – to St Custards or St Trinians. To little private ghettoes of etiquette and learning. They're going anywhere my pupils are not. Sixty per cent of this royal borough.

Some are ferried in fat jeeps and tanks. Is that Nigel Molesworth gazing glumly from that plump juggernaut?

Two worlds. 'Twas ever thus. I'm stuck in both.

Like this evening I'm stuck at a chic soiree, pretending I'm not a teacher. I might be a loan shark, a lollipop man, a mortician – or Charlie Watts.

"Teaching must be so fulfilling ... rewarding!"

Oh dear. I'll have to get drunk. But I must not rant.

"Is it true what they say about your school?"

"Erm ..." Where's that wine?

"Is it true about the drugs/knives/guns?" Glug.

"Didn't Tony Benn send his children to your school?" Glug. Glug.

"Can we send Ned/Hector/Rhapsody/Moon Unit to your school?"

Cutlery stops. All glare. Glug. Glug. Glug. Wife mimes "No!" I stay shtoom.

"I've seen them on our streets!" yells Mr Hillbilly. "Hooligans! A football mob ... indisciplined ... illiterate ... I blame the teachers ..."

I thought he might. Where's that Merlot gone? Wife again mimes "No".

"I've always believed passionately in the state system!" trills Mrs Hillbilly. "Never dreamed of going private ... can't sacrifice Hector to our principles ... he is delicate ... gifted ... he needs stretching ... stretching ... stretching." Glug. Glug. Glug.

"Is there a selection process?"

Wife seems to be doing semaphore. But I'm a glass too far. "The school's policy has always been less than vigorous!" I drone. "Apart from florid schizophrenics, proven multiple assassins, wolf children, Latin scholars and Chelsea fans, and anyone called Hector, most pass the interview."

Kick on shin from wife.

"Of course Hector should come to my school. All your children should! The only solution. Karl Marx said …" Massive whack on shin.

Exit ranting pursued by wife.

"Stretch him! I'll stretch that little blighter!"

Is it cos I's rubbish?

Published 9 February 2006

Top schools "exclude" poorer students, reports the Sutton Trust. Their findings "starkly underline the extent of the social divide". Twas ever so.

In my day it was called the 11-plus. If you were "good with your brains" you went to grammar school. "Good with your hands" and you went to technical school.

The other 90% went to secondary modern school. My dad said if I failed I would be rubbish and a derelict. I passed. Hurrah! Off I went to the RGS High Wycombe.

I never spoke to my village chums again. They became teddy boys and cudgelled our brains. They were good with their hands.

Buckinghamshire is still run thus. They top league tables. Never again, I thought.

My comprehensive school used to take all God's children. Now we just go through the motions. We admit them. And then we select them. Then we exclude them.

It's called streaming. You have to. League tables. A–Cs go into top stream. Ds get hothoused. The rest – about 55% – go into the "not top" stream. Foundation. An exclusion zone.

Here they come – my not top 9th year. Thirty of them. E grades to unclassifieds.

The lost and luckless of west London. From war zone and famine and blight and B&B and hostel and embassy and caravan. Lost.

Shaka's lost his marbles. Dragana's lost her family. Geena never had one. Finbar's lost his temper. Crumlin's lost his hat and Billy Boy's just lost.

Not waving just drowning. Meanwhile Olga reads Kundera. And Shkelzen reads advanced physics. They didn't do well in the MidYIS English test – what with coming from Prague and Albania.

There's 14 SEN pupils and a dozen EAL. There's no support teachers. Who cares, eh? Why don't we just pen them in the north playground and throw them turkey twizzlers. Or put them in the stocks with pointy D caps? The derelicts.

We're having a rather good lesson when Thomas from top stream appears.

"Who are these fuckwits?" he yells.

"You're foundation! You're rubbish you are!"

I am furious. So's the class

"Oi, sir, 'e's dissin' us !"says Fin. "I might have to rip his lungs out! Posh git!" Finbar is good with his hands. I suggest that Thomas leaves while he can still breathe.

"D'you take the rubbish cos you're a rubbish teacher?"

I'm on Fin's side. He goes. Divide and rule. The latest white paper will surely facilitate these things.

This is what we find

Published 28 June 2007

"Pioneering" researchers at the Institute of Education – after years of toil – have just published their findings.

The rich do better than the poor! Do they get paid for this?

The middle class do better than the working class! I pick self off floor.

Boys are dimmer than girls! Holy smoke!

Their fates are sealed after 3 years. The Jesuits needed seven! New Labour's worse! What grim findings. And mighty dull. Do they have degrees in The bleedin' obvious? We know these things.

Look at my 10th year. Let us consider exhibit A.

Crumlin. Ronald, 15. Poor. Working class. Male.

He's over there grunting at a poem whose ambiguities make him want to hit things.

Crumlin lives in a box at the top of King Hell Mansions. With his frazzled mother and antic brother and a wolf called Brains. There's no father or books or silence or space or privacy or stimulation. "'Cept when I was dropped on me 'ead!"

No one told the infant Crumlin stories as he slumbered. "'Cept for that Hungry Caterpillar."

He'd go Asbo if it weren't for the football. He wanders the world with the ball in the bag. The Tesco bag. He perfects his skills under the Westway or by inner city walls – or in my lessons.

Crumlin is bright – in the wrong things. He's a grade E and Level 3. So it goes.

Let us now consider exhibit B.

Bland. Rhapsody, 15. Rich. Middle class. Female.

She's over there gazing at the poem whose ambiguities delight her. She lives in a leafy West London with her liberal lawyer parents. They told the infant Bland many stories as she slumbered. She's been nourished on wheat germ and fish oil and broccoli and bits of Bach and whale songs in the womb and books and silence and space and much stimulation.

Rhapsody is bright in the right things. Grade A* and Level 10. So it goes.

We don't need these researchers.

But still they excavate the bleedin' obvious. They still have findings. They find that grammar schools do better than inner city comps and SATs and testing and targets and tables are stressful and destructive and small classes are good and rain falls downwards and turkey twizzlers make you fat and drugs make you daft and boys hit things.

And that Ronald Crumlin will never go to a university.

Any fule kno. I found out long ago. Crumlin too. He found out things when he was three. We're "pioneering". And we're both available to flog our cut-price findings at a PowerPoint near you.

Old school ties

Published 8 November 2007

Recent research reveals that Class Still Rules. Fewer working class children now go to university than in the 1950s. Comprehensive schools have changed nothing. I can confirm these cheerless findings with recent research of my own. A visit to my old school – the Royal Grammar School,

High Wycombe – after over 40 years. I left the infernal inner city for the rolling Chiltern Hills, for the 1950s…

I walk up the hill which leads to the school. I pass schoolboys dawdling happily down. Like we did. In their blue and maroon uniforms and wonky ties. Like ours were. Except for the long trousers. We sported rather fetching shorts. They have the same haircuts. The Pudding Bowl, Golf Divot, the Teddy Boy and, the Nigel Molesworth.

The 11-plus boys – cherry-picked and university-bound. Just like I was.

Is that my old chum Rumble with the Eddie Cochran hair? I pass the place where he told me that Buddy Holly had died. "It doesn't matter anymore," we sang in his honour.

Suddenly there it is! My old school. It's hardly changed

The sun falls over burnished classroom windows. Who are those shadows in the mist? My old teachers? With their Brylcreemed skulls and grim moustaches and gravitas and gowns.

Is that Sam Morgan still threatening clots with the cane?

"It's cold today – it might sting more, Willie!!"

Is that "Chunk" Jones blaspheming at my tenses?

"I'd rather teach a vegetable than you Whitwham!"

A lovely, daft, unfair, small world. I left it to change it. I left to teach the other 90 per cent. Off I went to teach in the inner city comprehensive. You couldn't do anything else. That ghetto of privilege had to go.

But sometimes I miss it. Sometimes I wish I were teaching The Lucy poems to Nigel Molesworth instead of barking out *Stig of the Dump* at Attila Dervish and Ronald Crumlin. Did I get it wrong? Of course not. Did things change? Of course not.

Not after 50 years. After boatloads of pedagogical mumbo jumbo. After Structuralists and Psycholinguists and Mixed Ability and Psychotic Phonics and a million government initiatives and a trillion droning workshops. The Berlin Wall came down but not the RGS High Wycombe…

Mist falls. Two boys with satchels stand outside the tuck shop. It could be the 1956. It could be Rumble and me.

Or could it be Crumlin and Dervish?

I wish. Never.

Educational apartheid

Published 31 January 2008

"Private schools fuel educational apartheid!" says Dr Anthony Seldom. Who he? Headmaster of a private school. Erm? Wellington College – £25 grand a go. And the remedy? Shoot self? Abolish private schools? Never. Private schools are the best.

"Best teachers, best pupils, best university places." And often rich.

State schools are less good. Duff teachers, feral pupils and few university places. And often poor.

Full of paupers. Naughty paupers. Hooligan paupers.

We all need the help of private school teachers. We need flagship academies sponsored by venture capitalists. Like Reg Varny – used car dealer and Creationist. Like flash John Nash, with "a passion for the underprivileged young". He should meet my hooligan Lunk when irked.

The Lord Adonis concurs – we need the "the DNA of private schools." Thus will our two nations be healed.

Not bad for the old tax break either – a cool £100 million a year.

Dear me. What glib thinking. Here's a couple more…

I take my lovely sixth form class to Cambridge. City of dreaming spires. Groves of academe. Students amble to lectures and tutorials and studies.

They are jolly and clever and smile – golden youth in the best days of their lives.

Sanctuary. Silence.

You go into cerebral trance.

Can we get in? Without those private teachers? Cut to…

Some of my lovely Key Skills class in London.

City of infernal night. Ladbroke Grove. A Grove of urban blight. They duck and weave from Westway to internet café. They are wired and sussed and rarely smile – the lost boys killing time. Dirty night falls on graffitied walls. A smudge-faced fellow stumbles across a red light. Cherry tops scream and ambulances howl. Shops flog rags and mags called *Nuts* and *Zoo* and one says "Di's a Whore" and another "Britney tops herself!" The moronic inferno rages.

No sanctuary. No silence. No language. You get a cerebral haemorrhage.

Two nations. "Educational apartheid" indeed.

And those remedies? Abolish private schools? Never going to happen. Those private school teachers? Have they ever taught my naughty paupers?

The brilliant Rhapsody? The benighted Lunk? My teacher chums do it really well. We don't need patrician patronage. We need dosh – that £100 million tax dodge for a start. For local community schools – with lovely libraries and Latin and very SMALL CLASSES.

Equal ops for all!

Published 8 May 2008

The exam season looms. At all levels. Most cope. Some don't. Like the student next to me during finals. Anglo saxon verse. He kept shaking. He sniffed his sleeves. Cocaine – nicked from the chemistry lab. A fine mind zonked, he just drew cartoons of Donald Duck. He failed.

I failed O level maths five times. All those cosines and obtuse angles did me in. My teacher hit me with a board duster. To no avail. I was still innumerate. Rubbish. It was genetic. I failed. A bit rough. Weren't we disabled? Physically? Emotionally? No one cared. Even for dyslexics. They just failed and sat at the back doing raffia work.

Now, thank goodness, things are kinder. If you've got dyslexia you get extra time. If you have physical/emotional difficulties you can have extra time – 92,000 pupils did last year. A level pupils get 45 minutes extra. Fair play to them.

But now there's concern that some pupils are trying it on. Their parents pay shrinks four grand to pronounce them "slow readers", "slow writers" – or "slow processors of information". Or a bit bonkers. That's half my class! Where do we draw the lines?

I propose the following criteria for my pupils.

Those with no parents, no English, no home and from war zones – 2 hours extra. Like Jiri from Albania.

Those with single parents who live in King Hell Mansions. No room. No books. No money and no sanctuary – 1 hour extra. Like Charlie Johnstone.

The terminally lazy. The relentlessly truanting. The partially stupid. The lost and bewildered and those concussed from football – half an hour extra. Like Ronald Crumlin. "I'm a bit dizzy, sir!"

The Toxic. Those on a diet of additives and Es and Kentucky Fried Dogburgers. Those poisoned by the lead under the Westway. Those with IQ shredding skunk habits – like Shaka Lynch. No extra time. It would make no difference. No entry. Save on the admin.

All boys – 10 minutes extra.

The Seriously Advantaged would have time taken off. Those with private tutors or pushy mums who do their children's coursework or buy answers off the net – half an hour less.

The privately educated. One hour less. No entry. No point. They can't not get A grades – unless they're cretins. Just let them proceed straight to their Oxbridge college. Save on the admin.

All girls – their rich interior worlds give them an unfair advantage – 10 minutes less.

There we go. That should do it. Equal ops for all!

Living in the city

Published 5 June 2008

My teacher chums in the shires sometimes wonder why I'm still in an inner city school. It sounds like a loony bin. Some kind of correctional facility for florid delinquents. They say that it's cushier in the shires. I could be doing Latin in the shades of academe. I could be watching cricket in the evening sun. Surely I've had enough of my illustrious hooligans? Of Mad Shaka skunked out of his wits and Attila Dervish falling out of windows and of the clunking Sidney Lunk? Of all that urban blight?

Well, sometimes, yes. But, most times, not at all.

It's never dull. And often rather thrilling.

Take my top 11th year. There's nothing better than an inner city state school top stream 11th year. Especially from London. They're such a rich mix and so variously clever. All those cultures and classes and tribes coming at you. Asylum seekers, goths, hip-hoppers, rastas, indie boys and Jeff Buckley girls – and I don't know what. All inner city sussed. You can't buy it. They're full of such quick wit. They're up for anything – Salinger, Pelecanos, Lorca, the Arctic Monkeys and Sir Thomas Wyatt. Even the stern TS Eliot. A London boy.

"Let us go through half deserted streets… muttering streets…"

"Like Ladbroke Grove, sir!" Not half.

And Shakespeare – another London scribe. We went to the Roundhouse to see the recent Histories. They loved them. They got them. Many knew too well about bloody civil strife. Magda saw it in Serbia. Vladimir saw it in Chechnya. And some see it in the inner city streets.

We even did the dull and shrinking syllabus. They're doing the GCSE exam now. They're much too good for all those impertinent questions. They'll do well.

Maybe my chums have been reading too much of the prim Melanie Phillips and her precious ilk. There's a lot of them about. They seem to see London as Alexander Pope saw it in *The Dunciad*. They seem to loathe variety and pine for the thin gruel of a moribund monoculture. Dear me. They don't seem too keen on my pupils.

Well, I think they're rather magical. It's about time they were celebrated. They're London's finest. I'll miss them. I hope they come back in my 6th form. We could read anything. We might even do a bit of Latin. New Mayor Boris is rather keen on it. Who knows? Crumlin could be pondering Catullus and Lunk could be knee deep in Virgil. He'd like the punch-ups.

The shires can wait. The inner city keeps you sharp. It refreshes those parts the shires can't always reach...

Down to 'The Wire'

Published 11 June 2008

"Some state pupils are unteachable!" thunders ex-Rear Admiral Chris Parry. That would be Dave Mania and Attila Dervish – presently failing something in a hall. Some parents aren't much better. He met some once. "They're ignorant!" His solutions?

"Schools need good teachers!"

There's no fooling this sea-faring fellow – now Chief of Independent Schools. His hard-earned insights scar the mind. Education can't be free! He elucidates.

"If you give rifles to Afghanis they give them to the Taliban!"

Absolutely. Is he the new Peter Cook? There's more.

"How can you get an Oxford graduate out that group?"

Indeed. Mania and Dervish aren't going to any dreaming spires. Wormwood Scrubs turrets more like. I blame me. Well, maybe not...

"Some teachers are wonderful!" he drones. Some Rear Admirals aren't. He's not alone. Other gurus, unencumbered by any relevant experience, are also keen to address the Big Issues. Knife crime? "Show them pictures of stabbings!" say ministers.

"My goodness," says Psycho Charlie, "what a horrid sight! I must surely desist!" The unemployed? "Send them to boot camps!" says Tory thinker Chris Grayling.

It's time they all shut up and watched *The Wire*. The best TV programme ever. Set in Baltimore, it's created by journalist David Simon and former cop and teacher Ed Burns. Its acting is stunning. It's tough, compassionate, complex – and hugely entertaining. Are you watching it? It's hidden away on the FX channel. You need to get it on DVD. Or, better, get your management to show it instead of those twilight "brain gym" workshops. Start with Series 4 – set in an inner-city middle school. It's all there. Teachers drudging away against a chorus of clots. Plodding through the "scam of SATs" and "junking the stats" to keep management, mayors and ministers sweet. This series explores class, race, poverty, gangs, absent fathers, stolen childhoods and much else – with unflinching empathy and no preaching. And our need for an underclass. Our need to fail Dave Mania and Attila Dervish. Those "unteachables" – who are rarely stupid, just deeply damaged.

"They will learn. It's just a question of where!" says Ed Burns. They learn terrible things. They will have fates like Greek tragedies. They will break your hearts. You will never respond again to gang killings with such dumb exasperation. You will never again dismiss those "unteachables" with such facile ease.

Nor, hopefully, will some Rear Admirals.

Yes we can!

Published 20 November 2008

My daughter rings up from America, dizzy with happiness – "Fantastic! Whooh!"

She's in Grant Park, Chicago, listening to Obama's victory speech. I'm in London, listening to it too. I'm dizzy too – and a bit moist eyed. It is fantastic.

"Yes we can!" I hear. "Wheh! Heh!" she goes.

She's a student there. She teaches in a primary school. She leaves the pampered, privileged campus for the crumbling wastelands of the Southside. A Black ghetto. She's teaching seven-year-olds to read and write. One little girl struggles to read. Why? She can't see the letters. Why?

No glasses. No money for glasses. Another little girl can't write. Why? No paper. School can't afford it. It can kill all hope.

But not right now. Now we can believe in American Dreams and Promised Lands and in what Lincoln called our "better angels".

My daughter must feel like we did in the 60s.

A time of real hope. "A Change Is Gonna Come", as Sam Cooke sang. We teachers were going to change the world. It's why I took up this lark.

Well, my generation blew it. It didn't get better. It seems to have got worse – especially education. Many of my chums lost all hope and retreated into a cynicism that was corrosive.

"NO WE CAN'T – BECAUSE WE DIDN'T!"

Well, not tonight. Obama mugs despair and doubt.

"New America! New Deal! This is our moment!"

Isn't the rhetoric a bit foggy? Of course it is. And it connects like a Springsteen song. But won't the Big Oil boys, the Neo Cons and Fox News be out to get him? Probably. But he's too cool – in every sense. Too fast for them. And hasn't he inherited the toxic legacy of George Bush? Two divided nations. Surely he can't heal such deep wounds? He cannot walk on water. Probably not.

No matter. Right now we feel a bit better. Not just in Chicago. In London too. My pupils are just buzzing. "Yesss!" goes the common cry. "He the man!" says Little Kevin. "He cool!" says Finbar. "He so fit!" says Chanteuse. "I want a puppy too!" says Sabrina. Only Shaka breaks our mood – with a chilling dread. "Good for him, but he's only going to get shot anyway!"

I gaze round the room. Here where class is still destiny. Maybe change can come. Maybe it's our time. Maybe my pupils can escape. My daughter's pupils are buzzing too.

"The White House ain't the White House no more! It's the Crib!" says that girl with no glasses. Fantastic! Whooh! Now where's that Sam Cooke song?

Oxbridge interviews

Published 4 December 2008

Luke has an interview next week at Cambridge. We've been practising for it. I might not be the best person for this. I once had an interview at Cambridge and I've still got the scars. It was December 1962.

I'm standing outside a door in Peterhouse College. I'm about to be interviewed by Mr Amis. That's Kingsley Amis the illustrious satirist. The scourge of waffling clots. I could well be one. I am clinically shy, quaking in my Hush Puppies, and look daft. My apparel is by Sexual Desert, my hair by Medieval peasant, and my confidence in freefall. I hear wild music behind his door. Boogie Woogie music. Knock! Knock!

Nothing.

Knock! Knock!

"Do come in!"

I shuffle into near darkness. These must be the shades of Academe. There are books, bottles and a record player – and the world's most satirical man.

"Hello!" he may have said. He changes a record – an old 78. Jelly Roll Morton. Brothel music.

I lean pointlessly about and fall into a sofa.

"If you were on a long train journey what novel would you take?" says a voice from the shades.

"Erm. Lucky Jim?" Of course not.

"Wuthering Heights," I hear myself shriek. I've prepared some rather significant opinions on it – with my English teacher "Min".

I deliver them in a flat drone. I mumble them to bits of furniture. I seem to be swallowing marbles.

I address incest, necrophilia and orgasms. Just what a major satirist needs to hear from a callow virgin on a sofa. Mr Morton meanwhile addresses that "old jelly roll". Mr Amis seems keener on his profanities than my banalities.

He continues to drink and I continue not to think.

We are now two separate events. I am having a monologue at him – mistaking him for the kind of Fellow who gives a fig. My confidence now nil, I elect myself mute. The interview may have finished. I get up. We nearly shake hands. I shuffle out of a door. "Min" is informed that I am "woeful" – and "without obvious potential". I still wake up hearing these words.

Well, things have got better. Oxbridge now seem keener on state pupils like Luke. Those dreaming spires seem less of a nightmare and the interviews less of a trauma. Some of my pupils have got in.

I tell Luke, who is brilliant, not to prepare parrot answers.

We brush up on the Jacobeans, The Wire, the Arsenal midfield, Wordsworth's pantheism – and Jelly Roll Morton. I quote an admissions tutor. "Relax, be honest, be awake, look your interviewer in the eye and good luck."

Indeed. And avoid that Peterhouse college – and anyone called Amis...

Plenary

Reasons to be cheerful

And so ... class ... what can we finally glean from this slim tome? What key bullet points? Despite these many cheerless moments, there are many reasons to be cheerful. Let me put them on our blackboard.

1. The whole modern, managing, measuring, market-driven culture seems, like the City it seems to serve, to be in meltdown.
No one likes it. Its number is up. It kills the spirit and shrinks the soul. Are you listening at the back? Good. Thank you.

2. Small classes are the answer.
Any fule kno this.

3. Most teachers are terrific.
Against considerable odds. Leave them alone. Trust them. The classroom is theirs and should be immune to blundering interventions. And finally ... could you stay awake over there! That's better.

4. Most pupils are terrific.
Against considerable odds. Yes, many are fierce, troubled and irksome but so would you be. Plots and pogroms and wheezes hover over them like those monsters in Goya's 'Sleep of Reason', but to gratifyingly little effect. Trumped by the energy, speed and wit of my prize scamps. By the sheer intelligence of Luke, the calm of Cordelia, the volume of Decibelle, the frolics of Dervish, the visions of Shaka, the dullness of Lunk and even the absence of Charlie Johnstone. No system on earth can shrink them to a measurable outcome. Thank goodness.

And, finally, Ronald Crumlin. There are a lot of Crumlins. If you're not teaching Crumlins I can't see the point of teaching at all. There he is – concave of skull and shorn of hair with skew-whiff tie and half-mast trousers and the football in the Tesco's bag. Invincible. He's in detention for something or other. He's failed a target or fallen out of Mr Donut's classroom or asleep in Mr Vholes' assembly or off a chair with Ms Limpet the Freudian. Whatever. I'm afraid he might be terrifically sane. And a bit of a hero. An inner city Molesworth. A Huckleberry Finn even. Schooling? Education? It don't always take. It's like Huck's Aunt Sally who "wants to sivilise me and I don't want it!"

There he is, perched at the back. I regard his unquiet visage.
"Alright, then, sir?"
Well, yes, actually.
Pip! Pip! Pip!